Twenty-five Years
of Economic Development
1950 to 1975

Twenty-five Years of Economic Development 1950 to 1975

David Morawetz

Published for the World Bank

The Johns Hopkins University Press

Baltimore and London

*The views and interpretations in this book
are the author's and should not be attributed
to the World Bank, to its affiliated organizations, or to any individual acting in their
behalf.*

First paperback printing, September 1977
First clothbound printing, August 1978
Second paperback printing, August 1978

Library of Congress Cataloging in Publication Data:

Morawetz, David.
  Twenty-five years of economic development, 1950 to 1975.

  Bibliography: p. 103
  1. Underdeveloped areas—History. 2. Economic
development—History. I. Title.
HC59.7.M578   330.9'172'4   77–17243
ISBN 0–8018–2134–7
ISBN 0–8018–2092–8 paperback

Foreword

As the colonial era came to an end, development of the newly independent countries became a focus of world attention. The 1950s saw the establishment of targets for the economic growth of poor countries, the formulation of national development plans, and the emergence of the new field of development economics. Since then development programs have been adopted by practically all developing countries, and international organizations have regularly adopted global targets to guide efforts toward international cooperation.

After twenty-five years it is opportune to attempt a broad assessment of these efforts. To do so, Professor Morawetz has first reexamined the objectives of the developing countries and how they have changed over time. The difficulty of attempting social change and growth simultaneously in the conditions of the 1950s led to an emphasis on the acceleration of aggregate growth as a means of overcoming the "vicious circle of poverty," which led to an emphasis on increased GNP as a measure of success in development. This simple perception has now been replaced by a more complex statement of social objectives, which recognizes that economic growth is a necessary but not a sufficient condition for social progress and that more direct attention should be given to the welfare of the poorest groups.

Morawetz shows that although the developing countries have on balance been remarkably successful in achieving growth, the distribution of its benefits among and within countries has been much less satisfactory. Rapid growth has created a new set of

v

distributional problems for the more successful countries, but for more than a billion people in more stagnant economies increasing production is still the main requirement for reducing poverty. Morawetz's assessment of a quarter century of experience shows that growth has been possible under a wide variety of circumstances, but he warns against concluding that poverty has been correspondingly alleviated.

The World Bank gives high priority in its research program to the evaluation of development experience, which is the foundation for improvements in analysis and policymaking. Professor Morawetz was invited by the Bank to undertake the present study, which makes extensive use of Bank materials as well as other sources. Although he has had extensive discussions with Bank staff members, the design of the study and the conclusions reached are entirely his own.

HOLLIS B. CHENERY
Vice President, Development Policy

Contents

TABLES

Acknowledgments

I AM ESPECIALLY INDEBTED to Helen Hughes and Donald Keesing, who went through two earlier versions of the study with a fine-tooth comb, improving it greatly. I wish to thank the following members of the World Bank staff for enjoyable discussions on the state of the world in 1950, for help with the literature and data in their fields of expertise, and for comments on an earlier draft; my debt to them, too, is enormous: John H. Adler, Hari Aggarwal, Montek Ahluwalia, Dragoslav Avramovic, Bela Balassa, Boris Blazic-Metzner, Shahid Javed Burki, Nicholas Carter, Hollis Chenery, Barend de Vries, Fredrick Golladay, James Greene, Mahbub ul Haq, Ralph Hofmeister, Thomas Hutcheson, Paul Isenman, Douglas Keare, Benjamin King, Thomas Klein, Mark Leiserson, Ian M. D. Little, Göran Ohlin, Guy Pfeffermann, Bertrand Renaud, Shlomo Reutlinger, Götz Schreiber, Marcelo Selowsky, John Shilling, John Simmons, Shamsher Singh, Alexander Stevenson, Ardy Stoutjesdijk, Paul Streeten, Marinus van der Mel, and S. Venkitaramanan. From outside the World Bank, I was fortunate to receive helpful comments from Robert Asher, P. T. Bauer, Donald Daly, and Frank Meissner. The fact that I had access to the data tapes of the World Bank's economic and social data bank facilitated the task greatly. Last, but certainly not least, Komola Ghose, Ben Sands, and Dirk Zijlstra provided sterling research assistance, and Mr. Zijlstra prepared the Appendix tables. The final manuscript was edited by Goddard W. Winterbottom; Brian J. Svikhart supervised production of the book. I alone am responsible for all views expressed.

DAVID MORAWETZ

March 1977

*Twenty-five Years
of Economic Development
1950 to 1975*

Introduction

WHAT HAS BEEN THE EXPERIENCE of developing countries with
economic development over the past quarter of a century? Has
development "succeeded" or "failed"? In either case, what lessons
can be learned from the experience of the past, and what questions are raised for the future? The aim of this study is to take a
first cut at assembling and evaluating some of the evidence bearing on these questions. The study does not attempt to survey the
history of ideas about development,[1] nor does it try to identify
patterns of development and structural change.[2]

"Developing countries" are defined throughout the study as
including all of Asia (except Japan), Africa (except South
Africa), and Latin America, but as excluding all of Europe (although several countries in eastern and southern Europe are often
considered to be developing countries). Because of the lack of
comparable data, Cuba, North Korea, and Mongolia are omitted
throughout. At the regional level, figures for East Asia always
exclude the People's Republic of China (hereinafter simply
"China"), which, because of its size, is treated as a separate
region. The detailed country-level data on which the summary
text tables are based are presented in the tables in the Statistical
Appendix.

1. On development ideas from Adam Smith to World War II, see Robbins [1968] and Arndt [1972]. On postwar developments, see Adler [1972],
Adelman [1975], Ranis [1976], Yotopoulos and Nugent [1976], and
Streeten [1977a].
2. See, for example, Kuznets [1965, 1967, and 1971], Chenery [1975
and 1976], and Chenery and Syrquin [1975].

3

Estimates of gross national product, or GNP, per capita in developing countries must be treated with caution. In particular, the use of exchange rates rather than purchasing-power parities [3] to convert estimates in national currencies to a single common denominator (usually U.S. dollars) seriously overstates the real income gap separating rich and poor nations. For example, the conventional statistics converted on the basis of exchange rates indicate that more than 1 billion people in the developing world (610 million in India alone) had an average per capita GNP of $140 or less in 1975.[4] Yet anyone who travels to work by public transport in North America or western Europe spends more than this sum each year in bus or train fares alone. If the per capita GNP figure is supposed to mean that Indians are consuming each year an amount of goods and services no larger than could be bought in the United States for $140, most Indians are so poor that they could not possibly survive, let alone increase their numbers. But if the per capita GNP figure does not mean this, it is not clear what it does mean.[5]

This example gives a first indication that the bias inherent in the conventional figures is indeed serious. The most recently available evidence on the subject indicates that, for the poorest countries, purchasing-power parity estimates of per capita incomes tend to be just over three times as great as conventional estimates [Kravis, Heston, and Summers 1977]. Thus, India's per capita income estimated on a basis of purchasing-power parities

3. The purchasing-power parity doctrine was first invoked in the period of the Napoleonic wars, it was christened by Cassel [1918] during World War I, and it has been resurrected at least twice since World War II. For references to the early literature, see Gilbert and Kravis [1954], Haberler [1961], and Balassa [1964a]. Some of the more recent writings on the subject are by Usher [1968], Clague and Tanzi [1972], Daly [1972], Balassa [1973], and Hulsman-Vejsová [1975]. Kravis and others [1975] and Kravis, Heston, and Summers [1977 and 1977a] present the preliminary results of an ongoing attempt to estimate purchasing-power parity GNPs for a large number of countries. On some other problems with using GNP as an indicator of welfare, see, for example, Baster [1972], Kuznets [1972a], Seers [1972], Tobin and Nordhaus [1972], and Barlow [1977].
4. All dollar figures in this book refer to U.S. dollars.
5. This formulation of the problem is similar to that of Usher [1968].

comes out at more than $450, instead of $140 as conventionally measured.[6]

Fortunately, it seems that this measurement problem may be less important when examining the growth of a particular country over time,[7] as is done in most parts of this study, than in comparisons among countries at a point in time, which is done mainly in the section on "The Gap." It would be a pity to throw out the baby with the bath water; the available data on GNP and its growth rate are better than nothing.[8] Nevertheless, to minimize distortions resulting from the use of conventional GNP measurements, an attempt is made in this study to complement the analysis of growth rates in GNP per capita with evaluations of progress on other, more tangible indicators such as supply of nutrition, life expectancy, and literacy wherever this is possible.

6. As the per capita income of the country rises, the conversion factor used to derive purchasing-power parity estimates from conventional estimates tends to fall. This is because the price of nontraded goods, mainly personal services, tends to be higher in rich countries than in poor ones, and it explains why the use of conventional estimates significantly overstates the size of the gap between rich and poor nations. For a fuller statement of this argument see, for example, Balassa [1964a] and Kravis, Heston, and Summers [1977].

7. In the absence of historical data on purchasing-power parity GNPs, it is not yet possible to be certain on this point. For some relevant theoretical considerations, see Bhagwati and Hansen [1972], Kravis, Heston, and Summers [1977 and 1977a], and Strout [1977].

8. Nothing, or close to nothing, is what in 1950 an investigator of "Twenty-five Years of Economic Development: 1925 to 1950" would have had as a data base.

1

The Changing Objectives
of Development

AN ATTEMPT TO EVALUATE THE DEVELOPMENT EXPERIENCE
since 1950 needs first to examine the objectives to which development efforts have been directed. Largely as a result of changes in
perceptions in the developing countries themselves, since the early
1970s there has been a sharp shift in these objectives. It is now
considered that maximization of GNP per capita is too narrow an
aim and that other aims related to poverty reduction need to be
considered as well: improving income distribution, increasing
employment, fulfilling "basic needs."

Some observers have tended to regard this movement as just
one more fashion in a fashion-prone discipline. I would argue,
however, that the discovery of these additional objectives is in fact
a rediscovery of issues that were quite central in the writing on
economic development just after World War II. Seen in this historical context, the recent heightened concern with eradication of
poverty is not likely to be just another fad. On the contrary,
in the long term it is the narrow preoccupation of the late
1950s and 1960s with growth in average per capita income
that, although it had its reasons and even its benefits, may turn out
to be the passing fashion.

The early postwar concern with wider objectives than simply

growth is not difficult to document, since most of the literature of that time, both practical and theoretical, states the objectives of development in terms remarkably similar to those used today. The first plan in a developing country—that of India in 1952—aimed at "maximum production, full employment, the attainment of economic equality and social justice." [1] The first World Bank mission to a developing country—to Colombia in 1950—stated its objectives in terms of fulfillment of "basic human needs." [2] Much of the early economic literature of the United Nations was devoted to the subject of unemployment.[3] And in 1954, Kuznets [1955] devoted his presidential address to the American Economic Association to the subject "Economic Growth and Income Inequality." [4]

The problem in these early days was that it was difficult to make any headway in solving development problems in the face of multiple objectives and interlocking "vicious circles." [5] What was needed was a grand simplification that would break the impasse; it was Lewis [1954 and 1955] who provided it. In *The Theory of Economic Growth,* Lewis set the tone for the next fifteen years when he began: "First it should be noted that our subject matter is growth, and not distribution" [1955, p. 9].[6] To

---

1. Government of India [1952, p. 8].

2. World Bank (mission to Colombia) [1950, pp. 353–56 and 614–15]. Staley, "the man who more than any other brought the theme of economic development into the American discussion" [Arndt 1972, p. 26], saw the objective of development as fulfilling "basic human wants or desires" [Staley 1954, p. 92]. In a paper written in 1954, Kuznets reviewed data on nutrition in rich and poor regions [Kuznets 1965]. For Viner [1952, p. 127] "reduction of mass poverty" was the central objective.

3. Mikesell [1954]. The United Nations also produced early reports on the world social situation; ECOSOC was the Economic *and Social* Council.

4. Forty years earlier, Pigou [1912 and 1920] placed heavy emphasis on income distribution in his seminal works on welfare economics.

5. See, for example, the editorial in the first issue of the first journal in development economics, *Economic Development and Cultural Change,* in 1952.

6. As often happens, the followers were more extreme than the innovator. Lewis himself was very much aware of the problems of using growth in per capita income as the sole indicator of development; *The Theory of Economic Growth* contains a fifteen-page appendix entitled

be sure, there were still governments and theorists who were concerned about objectives other than growth during this period.[7] But the view that prevailed during most of the late 1950s and 1960s was that the "trickle-down" mechanism would solve the poverty and income distribution problems if only growth were fast enough.

By the early 1970s a number of factors converged to dampen this optimism about growth. It became clear that rapid growth had been accompanied by increased regional or personal income inequalities in some countries (Pakistan, Nigeria, and Brazil, for example), and possibly by increased absolute poverty in some cases.[8] The tolerance for poverty and inequality seemed to be decreasing as the raised expectations of and for the poor remained unfulfilled.[9] And the evidence of China's remarkable success in development began to filter out to the rest of the world.[10]

"Is Economic Growth Desirable?" At about the same time as Lewis was writing, there was a strong resurgence of interest in growth problems in developed countries as well. At the meeting of the American Economic Association in 1955, ten of the eighteen sessions had the words "economic growth" in their titles [*American Economic Review,* May 1956].

7. See, for example, International Labour Office (hereinafter ILO) [1961], a 1962 paper of the Indian Planning Commission reproduced in Srinivasan and Bardhan [1974], Myint [1964], and Bhagwati [1966].

8. For a summary of the evidence, see the section Reduction of Poverty, below. Lewis himself was one of the first to sense the problem. "One disturbing factor must be set against the high rates of growth of output and investment on which we have been congratulating ourselves; namely the rising levels of unemployment in the underdeveloped countries. This cannot be documented because there are no reliable statistics of unemployment, but it is everywhere a cause of concern. The phenomenon is unexpected, since rapid growth and high investment ought not to increase unemployment but to reduce it" [Lewis 1965, p. 12].

9. Hirschman [1973]. A similar change in attitude took place during the industrial revolution in England when, for the first time, poverty became "a problem to be solved" [Hartwell and others 1972, p. 20].

10. See, for example, Keesing [1975] and the references he cites. The China-India comparison had been a point of fascination for many in the field of economic development from the early 1950s, see, for example, Malenbaum [1959] and Weisskopf [1975]. As late as 1965 at least one scholarly observer could still conclude: "The performance of China's economy . . . has been grossly exaggerated. . . . With respect to com-

As a result, governments and theoreticians relearned what they had known earlier—that economic development must surely mean not only growth in average per capita income but also reduction of poverty.

---

parative growth rates in India and China, let us be more skeptical in the future than we have been in the past" [Klein 1965, pp. 38–39].

2

Growth

How RAPIDLY were GNP per capita and population expected to grow in 1950, and how has their actual growth compared with these expectations?

Growth in GNP per Capita

Until 1950 there had been little serious thinking on the growth prospects of "backward areas." The industrialized countries were just getting over their concern with recovery from the war,[1] and the IBRD was still occupied with reconstruction in Europe rather than development in Africa, Asia, and Latin America. There was as yet probably no university course on economic development, there was no development journal, and only a handful of scholarly works had been devoted to the subject.[2]

---

1. The American Economic Association's early postwar discussions of "economic problems of foreign areas" were devoted to Germany, Britain, Japan, and China. With memories of the post-1918 experience clear, Germany was a particular worry: "[F]or the next couple of decades we are going to be plagued with the German economic problem" [Hoover 1946, p. 649].
2. For example, Rosenstein-Rodan [1943], Mandelbaum [1945], Baran [1952], and Viner [1952]. Most of the earliest literature was concerned with the development of southeastern Europe.

The few people who had thought about the prospects for what were soon to be called "underdeveloped countries" did not hold out high hopes for the short- to medium-term future. After all, the industrialized nations, in their long period of economic growth unparalleled in world history, had managed to increase per capita income by only about 2 percent a year [Kuznets 1967]. There was no reason to expect that the underdeveloped countries, many of which had experienced no growth for millennia, would do any better.[3] On the contrary, in the face of significant advances in disease eradication and with many of the cultural, institutional, and economic preconditions for growth missing, economists were concerned whether these countries could make the minimum critical effort needed for economic growth to exceed population growth.[4] It is against this background of low historical growth rates and low expectations for the future that the actual growth performance of developing countries since 1950 needs to be seen.

The growth performance of developing countries during 1950–75 is marked by three outstanding characteristics: the rapid average growth rate, the wide diversity of experience, and the increasing disparity between richer and poorer developing countries.

The GNP per capita of the developing countries as a group grew at an average rate of 3.4 percent a year during 1950–75 (see Table 1). This was faster than either the developing countries (Table 2) or the developed nations [Kuznets 1971] had grown in any comparable period before 1950 and exceeded both official goals and private expectations.

The high average growth rate masks a wide diversity of per-

3. By the arithmetic of compound interest, if the Indian average income per capita 2,000 years ago had been even $25 in today's prices (that is, close to or below subsistence level), and if it had grown at only 0.5 percent a year since then, today it would stand at over $300,000. In fact, historical reconstructions suggest that income per person in the Indian subcontinent probably stagnated between 1600 and 1900 and perhaps fell between 1900 and 1950 [Lipton 1977, p. 29]. Paintings on the inside walls of tombs near Luxor indicate that the way and standard of living of the Egyptian peasant have changed remarkably little in 5,000 years.

4. Lewis [1965]. For examples of relatively pessimistic predictions for particular countries, see World Bank [1950], Thorp [1951], Britnell [1953], and Ellsworth [1953].

Table 1. GNP per Capita and Its Annual Growth Rate, by Region, 1950–75

Region	Population, 1975 (millions) (1)	GNP per capita 1974 U.S. dollars		Annual growth rate, 1950–75 (percent) (4)
		1950 (2)	1975 (3)	
South Asia	830	85	132	1.7
Africa	384	170	308	2.4
Latin America	304	495	944	2.6
East Asia	312	130	341	3.9
China, People's Republic of	820	113	320	4.2
Middle East	81	460	1,660	5.2
Developing countries	2,732	160	375	3.4
Developing countries excluding China	1,912	187	400	3.0
Developed countries [a]	654	2,378	5,238	3.2

a. All OECD countries except Greece, Portugal, Spain, and Turkey.
Sources: Columns 1 and 3: data tapes of *World Bank Atlas* (1977). Column 2: estimated by applying growth rate of GDP per capita, 1950–60 (World Bank, *World Tables 1976*), to figures for 1960 GNP per capita (*Atlas* tapes). Column 4: Computed from columns 2 and 3.

formance. On one hand nine countries, with a combined population of 930 million people in 1975, grew at an average annual rate of 4.2 percent or better for the full period (Table 3), and a second group of nine countries, with 220 million people, grew at between 3 and 4 percent.[5] On the other hand, the large, poor countries of South Asia and many countries in Africa, with a total of some 1.1 billion people, grew in per capita income by less than 2 percent a year between 1950 and 1975. Thus, although it is true that per capita income has roughly trebled for some 33 percent of

5. This statement refers only to countries with a population of 1 million or more. The second group of nine contains Brazil, Somalia, Trinidad and Tobago, and Turkey (3.7 percent); Thailand (3.6 percent); Jordan and Sudan (3.3 percent); Syria (3.1 percent); and Nicaragua (3.0 percent). Among the southern European countries, which are not classified as developing countries in this study, Greece grew at 5.4 percent, Spain, at 5.1 percent, and Yugoslavia, at 4.7 percent.

Table 2.   Annual Growth Rate of GDP per Capita, Selected Countries, 1870–1975

(Percent)

Country	1870–1913 (1)	1913–50 (2)	1950–75 [a] (3)
Africa			
Egypt, Arab Republic of	n.a.	0.2	1.4
Ghana	n.a.	1.2	0.7
South Asia			
India	0.7	0.2	1.5
Pakistan	0.7	0.2	n.a.
East Asia			
China (Taiwan)	n.a.	0.7	5.3
Malaysia	n.a.	2.2	2.6
Philippines	n.a.	0.1	2.8
Latin America			
Argentina	1.5	0.7	1.9
Brazil	n.a.	2.4 [b]	3.7
Chile	n.a.	0.6	0.7
Colombia	n.a.	1.4	2.0
Mexico	1.2 [c]	1.2 [d]	2.7
Peru	n.a.	1.5	2.5
Other			
Greece	n.a.	−0.1	5.4
Spain	n.a.	−0.3	5.1
Yugoslavia	n.a.	0.9 [e]	4.7
Unweighted average	1.0	0.8	2.8 [f]

n.a. Not available.
a. Growth of GNP per capita.   c. 1877–1910.   e. 1909/12–50.
b. 1920–50.   d. 1910–50.   f. Weighted average = 2.0.
Sources: Columns 1 and 2: Maddison (1970), p. 32. Column 3: World Bank, *World Tables 1976,* and data tapes, *World Bank Atlas* (1977).

the people of the developing world during the past twenty-five years, it is also true that for another 40 percent the increase in per capita income has been only one or two dollars a year.

The disparity between richer and poorer developing countries has increased significantly since 1950, but it is not true at the aggregate level that the initially rich have got richer while the initially poor have got poorer. These twin facts may be seen from several different perspectives. At the regional level, in 1950 the average per capita income of the richest regions (Latin America and the Middle East) was five or six times that of the poorest (South Asia), whereas by 1975 the multiple for the Middle East

Table 3. GNP per Capita and Its Annual Growth Rate, Selected Countries, 1950–75

Country	Population, 1975 (millions) (1)	GNP per capita 1974 U.S. dollars 1950 (2)	GNP per capita 1974 U.S. dollars 1975 (3)	Annual growth rate, 1950–75 (percent) (4)
Eight most populous countries				
China, People's Republic of	820	113	320	4.2
India	610	95	139	1.5
Indonesia	132	103	169	2.0
Brazil	107	373	927	3.7
Bangladesh	79	105 [a]	103	−0.6 [b]
Nigeria	75	150	287	2.6
Pakistan	69	86 [a]	131	3.2 [b]
Mexico	60	562	1,092	2.7
Nine fastest-growing countries [c]				
Libyan Arab Republic	2	786 [d]	4,675	7.4
Iraq	11	283	1,180	5.9
China (Taiwan)	16	224	817	5.3
Korea, Republic of	34	146	504	5.1
Iran	34	384	1,321	5.1
Hong Kong	4	470	1,584	5.0
Jamaica	2	376	1,185	4.7
Israel	3	1,090	3,287	4.5
China, People's Republic of	820	113	320	4.2
Nine slowest-growing countries [c, e]				
Rwanda	4	119	81	−1.6
Burundi	4	117	91	−1.0
Upper Volta	6	99	87	−0.5
Madagascar	9	195	180	−0.3
Central African Empire	2	202	212	0.2
Bolivia	6	244	290	0.7
Chile	11	596	700	0.7
Ghana	10	354	427	0.7
Honduras	3	272	322	0.7

a. 1960.

b. 1960–75.

c. Countries with population of 1 million or more.

d. Real growth rates (and hence estimated 1950 GNP per capita figures) for oil-exporting countries depend heavily on the choice of base years in calculation of constant price national accounts. For example, in 1950 prices, Libya's 1950 GNP per capita was probably less than $100.

e. Excluding Khmer Republic (growth rate −1.4 percent), Lao People's Democratic Republic (0.3 percent), and Vietnam (0.5 percent).

Sources: Same as Table 1.

Table 4. GNP per Capita and Its Annual Growth Rate, by Income Group of Countries, 1950–75

Income group	Population, 1975 (millions) (1)	GNP per capita 1975 (1974 U.S. dollars) (2)	Annual growth rate, 1950-75 (percent) (3)
Lower-income countries	1,146	To $265	1.1
Middle-income countries	1,118	$266–$520	3.7
Middle-income countries excluding China	298		2.4
Upper–middle-income countries	370	$521–$1,075	3.4
Higher-income countries	100	$1,076+	5.2
Developing countries	2,732		3.4
Developing countries excluding China	1,912		3.0

Sources: Same as Table 1.

over South Asia had risen to thirteen, and that for Latin America was seven. But the relation between initial regional per capita income and subsequent regional growth rate is by no means uniform: initially rich Latin America grew relatively slowly, whereas initially poor China and East Asia grew more rapidly (Table 1).

If countries are divided into income groups on the basis of 1975 per capita income, the relation between income level and growth rate is almost uniform. On average, today's highest-income developing countries grew fastest, whereas the lower-income countries grew more slowly (Table 4).[6] But it is not surprising that there should be a positive correlation between terminal income and growth rates: over an extended period of time the relation is tautological.

Finally, at the level of the individual country, the ranking of eighty developing countries by GNP per capita remained remarkably stable between 1950 and 1975, while at the same time the

6. The country composition of the income groups is set out in the Appendix tables.

absolute disparity between the richest and the poorest developing nations increased by a factor of about three (Table 5).[7] As was true at the regional level, there seems to be no clear relation between initial income level and subsequent growth rate; the correlation between the two, though positive (0.17), is not significantly different from zero (see Figure 1).[8]

The way in which this growth performance measures up to private and official expectations may be gauged from a retrospective analysis of two projection exercises carried out some fifteen years ago. In 1960, Rosenstein-Rodan [1961] forecast the 1961–76 growth rates of GNP per capita and 1976 per capita income levels for sixty-six of today's developing countries. He expected that no country would grow as fast as 3 percent a year during the full fifteen-year period; in fact, eighteen did so. Further, in two-thirds of his cases, the actual GNP per capita figure for 1975 turned out to be at least 10 percent higher than his (inflation-adjusted) projection for 1976 (Table 6).[9]

(*Text continues on page 22.*)

7. The rank correlation coefficient is 0.91. Including only countries with a population of 1 million or more: (a) among the richest developing countries in 1975, only three (Iraq, Taiwan, and Turkey) were not in the top twenty in 1950; (b) among the poorest twenty developing countries in 1975, only four (Central African Empire, Kenya, Madagascar, and Uganda) were not among the bottom twenty in 1950; (c) only three countries (Iraq, Korea, and the Republic of China, referred to hereinafter as "Taiwan") managed to climb twenty places or more in the rankings during the period.

8. The correlation is similarly nonsignificant if the period 1960–75 is used instead of 1950–75. Chenery, Elkington, and Sims [1970] find a positive relationship between a country's income level and its growth rate for 1950–59 and 1960–65. But their sample of countries is rather different from the present one—it includes developed as well as developing nations —and the period covered is not identical.

9. In an otherwise critical comment on the Rosenstein-Rodan paper, Ranis [1962, p. 486] conceded that "no one in this field is in a better position (to make enlightened guesstimates of growth prospects) than Professor Rosenstein-Rodan himself." Ranis was concerned at the quality of the data, but did not comment on whether the projected growth rates seemed too high or too low—nor did Balassa [1964] in his comment on the study.

Figure 1. Relation between Annual Growth of GNP per Capita, 1950–75, and GNP per Capita, 1950

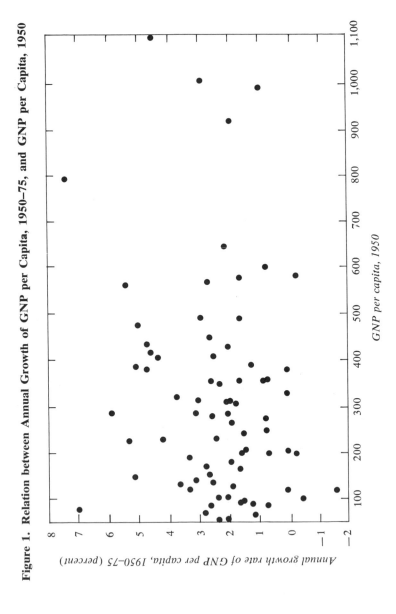

Table 5. Ranking of Developing Countries by GNP per Capita,
1950 and 1975

Country	GNP per capita [a]		Annual growth rate, 1950-75 (percent) (3)	Rank [b]		Difference (5)-(4) (6)
	1974 U.S. dollars			1950 (4)	1975 (5)	
	1950 (1)	1975 (2)				
Kuwait	19,160	10,590	−2.3	1	1	0
Libyan Arab Republic	786	4,675	7.4	6	2	+4
Israel	1,090	3,287	4.5	2	3	−1
Venezuela	992	2,045	2.9	3	4	−1
Hong Kong	470	1,584	5.0	13	5	+8
Argentina	907	1,464	1.9	5	6	−1
Iran	384	1,321	5.1	18	7	+11
Uruguay	978	1,220	0.9	4	8	−4
Jamaica	376	1,185	4.7	20	9	+11
Iraq	283	1,180	5.9	33	10	+23
Barbados	402	1,155	4.3	17	11	+6
Mexico	562	1,092	2.7	10	12	−2
Panama	484	977	2.9	12	13	−1
Brazil	373	927	3.7	21	14	+7
Fiji	571	842	1.6	9	15	−6
Costa Rica	445	834	2.6	14	16	−2
China (Taiwan)	224	817	5.3	43	17	+26
Turkey	316	793	3.7	28	18	+10
Peru	403	748	2.5	16	19	−3
Algeria	484	718	1.6	11	20	−9
Belize	424	700	2.0	15	21	−6
Chile	596	699	0.7	7	22	−15
Malaysia	350	665	2.6	25	23	+2
Dominican Republic	324	662	2.9	27	24	+3
Nicaragua	313	661	3.0	29	25	+4
Angola	226	623	4.2	42	26	+16
Syrian Arab Republic	283	604	3.1	35	27	+8
Guatemala	345	602	2.3	26	28	−2
Mauritius	575	533	−0.3	8	29	−21
Paraguay	354	525	1.6	22	30	−8
Guyana	383	512	1.2	19	31	−12
Colombia	308	510	2.0	31	32	−1
Korea, Republic of	146	504	5.1	54	33	+21
Ecuador	276	503	2.5	36	34	+2
Zambia	310	495	1.9	30	35	−5
Ivory Coast	283	460	2.0	34	36	−2

(Table continues on following page)

Table 5 (*continued*)

	GNP per capita [a]			Rank [b]		
	1974 U.S. dollars		*Annual growth rate, 1950–75*			*Differ-ence*
Country	*1950* (1)	*1975* (2)	*(percent)* (3)	*1950* (4)	*1975* (5)	(5)—(4) (6)
Congo, People's Republic of	303	461	1.7	32	37	−5
Morocco	353	435	0.8	24	38	−14
Swaziland	79	434	7.0	72	39	+33
Ghana	354	427	0.7	23	40	−17
Jordan	186	423	3.3	49	41	+8
El Salvador	263	418	1.9	38	42	−4
Papua New Guinea	229	412	2.3	41	43	−2
Senegal	238	341	1.5	40	44	−4
Philippines	168	340	2.8	51	45	+6
Honduras	272	322	0.7	37	46	−9
China, People's Republic of	113	320	4.2	62	47	+15
Thailand	132	319	3.6	57	48	+9
Botswana	141	300	3.1	55	49	+6
Bolivia	244	290	0.7	39	50	−11
Mauritania	200	288	1.5	46	51	−5
Nigeria	150	287	2.6	53	52	+1
Egypt, Arab Republic of	203	286	1.4	44	53	−9
Mozambique	177	284	1.9	50	54	−4
Sudan	118	267	3.3	60	55	+5
Cameroon	133	246	2.5	56	56	0
Togo	164	245	1.6	52	57	−5
Uganda	195	229	0.6	47	58	−11
Central African Empire	202	212	0.2	45	59	−14
Kenya	129	200	1.8	58	60	−2
Madagascar	194	180	−0.3	48	61	−13
Gambia, The	99	178	2.4	65	62	+3
Indonesia	103	169	2.0	63	63	0
Tanzania	84	160	2.6	71	64	+7
Zaïre	94	139	1.6	67	65	+2
India	95	138	1.5	66	66	0
Malawi	68	137	2.8	73	67	+6
Sri Lanka	90	134	1.6	68	68	0
Afghanistan	89	119	1.2	69	69	0
Nepal	87	102	0.7	70	70	0

Table 5 (*continued*)

Country	GNP per capita [a]		Annual growth rate, 1950–75 (percent) (3)	Rank [b]		
	1974 U.S. dollars			1950 (4)	1975 (5)	Difference (5)−(4) (6)
	1950 (1)	1975 (2)				
Burma	57	100	2.3	76	71	+5
Ethiopia	58	94	2.0	75	72	+3
Somalia	37	92	3.7	77	73	+4
Burundi	117	91	−1.0	61	74	−13
Upper Volta	99	87	−0.5	64	75	−11
Mali	67	86	1.1	74	76	−2
Rwanda	119	81	−1.6	59	77	−18

a. Simple correlation between columns 1 and 3=0.17.
b. Rank correlation between columns 4 and 5=0.91.
Sources: Columns 1–3: Same as Table 1. Columns 4–6: Calculated from columns 1 and 2.

Table 6. Outcome of Projections of Growth of GNP Made in the Early 1960s, Developing Countries, 1962–76 [a]

Projection	Number of countries			
	Projection too high	Projection correct [b]	Projection too low	Total
Rosenstein-Rodan (1961) projections of GNP per capita in 1976	17	6	43	66
Chenery-Strout projections of GNP growth rates, 1962–75				
Plan-based projections [c]	12	13	20	45
Upper-limit projections [d]	20	11	14	45

a. For the detailed country-by-country data, see Appendix Tables A4 and A5.
b. For Rosenstein-Rodan projections, up to 10 percent above or below actual GNP per capita figure for 1975. For Chenery-Strout projections, up to 0.5 percentage points above or below actual growth rate during 1962–75.
c. Projections based on the development plans of the major countries. Targets are described as "achievable with moderate improvements in development policies in relation to past experience." (Chenery and Strout, 1966, p. 711.)
d. "Our notion of the upper limit implies a probability of perhaps one in four that the given growth target and performance could be attained." (Chenery and Strout, 1966, p. 714.)
Sources: Computed from Rosenstein-Rodan (1961), p. 126, Chenery and Strout (1966, pp. 712–13), and data tapes, *World Bank Atlas* (1977).

The list of countries that Rosenstein-Rodan expected to be fast growers was rather different from what it would be today. Of the four nations that were expected to grow as fast as 3 percent a year during any five-year period, one was India, which was "in a take-off stage" and was expected to achieve self-sustaining growth "where aid is not required any more" by 1976 [pp. 113 and 116]. The other three were Burma, Argentina, and Hong Kong.

In another exercise carried out a few years later, Chenery and Strout [1966] projected 1962–75 growth rates of GNP—not GNP per capita—for forty-five developing countries. Their "plan-based" projections were described as being based on the development plans of the major countries, and as "achievable with moderate improvements in development policies" [p. 711]. A second set of "upper-limit" projections was described as implying "a probability of perhaps one in four that the given growth target and performance could be attained" [p. 714]. In the event, plan-based projections were attained or surpassed in three quarters of the forty-five cases, while even upper-limit projections were attained or surpassed more than half of the time (Table 6). The list of biggest disappointments—defined relative to the size of the disparity between projected and actual performance—again included India; it also included Chile, Egypt, Ghana, and Jordan. The biggest surprise successes included the oil-exporting countries, as well as Brazil, Kenya, Korea (which achieved double its projected 5 percent growth rate during the period), and Taiwan.[10]

---

10. An interim evaluation of the Chenery-Strout projections for the period up to 1970 was presented by Chenery and Carter [1973, 1973a]. Most other projections and targets of the early 1960s seem to have been attained or surpassed as well. In a book published for the Committee for International Economic Growth, Hoffman [1960, p. 10] proposed "that the nations of the world set for themselves the common task of assisting the people of the underdeveloped areas to increase the annual growth of their per capita income *from one to two percent each year* for the next ten years." When 5 percent growth in GNP (not GNP per capita) was chosen as the target for the first development decade, "it was chosen as an almost unmeetable challenge" [Lewis 1972, p. 415].

Growth in Population

Growth in GNP per capita is affected by growth in population as well as growth in GNP itself. Between 1950 and 1975 the population of the developing countries increased by 70 percent, or by more than 80 percent if China is excluded. Beginning in 1950 at 1.6 billion, it grew at an average annual rate of 2.1 percent during the 25 years (2.4 without China), reaching 2.7 billion by 1975. The annual rate of population growth was between 2 and 3 percent in all regions except China, where it was 1.5 percent (Table 7).

Twenty-five years ago it was not expected that population growth would become such a large problem in developing countries. As late as 1951 a U.N. projection assumed that between 1950 and 1980 the populations of Africa and Asia would grow at an annual rate of 0.7 to 1.3 percent.[11] The sharp surge was caused by the remarkable and largely unexpected success in reducing mortality, which, in turn, was brought about by higher standards of living, increased control of communicable diseases, and improved distribution of food in times of famine.

Whereas mortality rates have continued to decline in recent years, there are now signs that, following past experience in developed countries, fertility rates may be beginning to decline as well (Table 7). Nevertheless, because of current young age structures, even if fertility rates in the eight largest developing countries were to drop to replacement level tomorrow—in fact, they are not likely to reach that level for some years—their combined population would still be about 60 percent greater seventy years from now. Although a number of countries have recently shown an increased awareness of, and willingness to deal with, the problem, the process of reducing population growth is likely to continue to be a long, slow one.[12]

11. Cited in Pearson Report [1969].

12. It is unfortunately not possible in this brief review to discuss the complex, two-way relationship between population growth and economic development. For an excellent introduction to the voluminous literature on the subject, see Cassen [1976].

Table 7. Population Growth Rates and Crude Birthrates, Regions and Selected Countries, 1950–75

Region or country	Population (millions)		Annual population growth rate (percent)			Estimated annual crude birthrate (per thousand)	
	1950 (1)	1975 (2)	1950–60 (3)	1960–75 (4)	1950–75 (5)	1955 (6)	c1974 (7)
China, People's Republic of	560	820	1.4	1.6	1.5	32	26
South Asia	482	830	1.9	2.4	2.1	45	38
East Asia	171	312	2.6	2.4	2.4		
Africa	209	384	2.2	2.5	2.4	48	46
Latin America	150	304	2.8	2.8	2.8	43	38
Middle East	34	81	3.0	3.0	3.0	n.a.	n.a.
Developing countries	1,606	2,732	2.1	2.1	2.1	43	37
Developing countries excluding China	1,046	1,912	2.4	2.4	2.4	45	40
Developed countries	500	654	1.3	0.8	1.0	23	18

Eight most populous countries

China, People's Republic of	560	820	1.4	1.6	1.5	32	26
India	358	610	1.8	2.3	2.1	43	36
Indonesia	77	132	2.1	2.1	2.1	46	40
Brazil	52	107	3.0	2.8	2.9	41	38
Bangladesh	—ᵃ	79	n.a.	2.5	n.a.	49	49
Nigeria	43	75	1.9	2.5	2.2	49	49
Pakistan	—ᵃ	69	n.a.	2.9	n.a.	49	47
Mexico	26	60	3.2	3.4	3.3	46	41

n.a. Not available.

a. Total population of Pakistan and Bangladesh in 1950 was 80 million.

Sources: Columns 1–5: computed from data tapes, *World Bank Atlas* (1977). Columns 6–7: unpublished data, World Bank.

The Gap between Rich and Poor Countries

> *The widening gap between the*
> *developed and developing countries*
> *has become a central issue of our time.*
>
> PEARSON REPORT [*1969, p. 1*]

The caution concerning the doubtful validity of conventional GNP statistics for intercountry comparisons is particularly relevant in an examination of the gap between rich and poor nations. Once historical data on purchasing-power parity GNPs become available, the trend in the gap may appear to be quite different from that discussed below.

Although during 1950–75 the per capita incomes (as conventionally measured) of the developing countries were growing faster than ever before, so too were those of the developed countries. As a result, the gap between the rich and the poor nations, which had been increasing for 100 to 150 years [Kuznets 1965], continued to widen.

The relative gap

Since the developing and developed countries grew in per capita income at almost identical rates during 1950–75 (Table 1), the per capita income of the developing countries as a proportion of that of the developed countries stayed fairly constant, at around 7 to 8 percent. In China, East Asia, and particularly in the Middle East, the relative gap narrowed somewhat, whereas in South Asia, Africa, and Latin America it widened.

The absolute gap

In 1950 the average GNP per capita of the OECD countries (in conventional 1974 dollars) was $2,191 greater than that of the developing countries. By 1975 this difference had more than doubled, to $4,839 (Table 8). There is no single region in which the absolute gap did not at least double. Furthermore, apart from oil-rich Libya, not a single developing country for which data are

Table 8. The Relative and Absolute Gaps in GNP per Capita, by Region, 1950–75

	Relative gap [a] (*percent*)		Absolute gap [b] (*1974 U.S. dollars*)	
Region	1950	1975	1950	1975
South Asia	3.6	2.5	2,293	5,106
Africa	7.1	5.9	2,208	4,930
East Asia	5.5	6.5 [c]	2,248	4,897
China, People's Republic of	4.8	6.1 [c]	2,265	4,918
Latin America	20.8	18.0	1,883	4,294
Middle East	19.3	31.7 [c]	1,918	3,578
Developing countries	6.7	7.2 [c]	2,218	4,863
Developing countries excluding China	7.9	7.6	2,191	4,837

a. Relative gap is GNP per capita of region as percent of GNP per capita of the OECD countries.

b. Absolute gap is GNP per capita of the OECD countries ($2,378 in 1950, $5,338 in 1975) less GNP per capita of the region.

c. Relative gap decreased, 1950–75.

Sources: Computed from data tapes, *World Bank Atlas* (1977), and World Bank, *World Tables 1976.*

available for 1950 managed to narrow the absolute gap even slightly during the full twenty-five–year period.[13] Even in fast-growing Korea and Taiwan the absolute gap doubled.

This remarkable situation is the result of the simple algebra of gaps. In brief, a poor country growing faster than a rich one

13. Intuitively, it seems that some of the other oil-exporting countries must surely have narrowed the absolute gap as well. This highlights a problem existing throughout this and any other study that is based on *real* growth rates. In measuring a nation's increase in GNP, real growth rates— as they are usually calculated—abstract from price effects. The implicit assumption is that, in the long run, a country's consumption possibilities (and hence its economic welfare) are determined by its physical volume of production. Yet for some countries, and in particular for the oil exporters, the change over time in the relative prices of their principal products may be at least as important in determining national consumption possibilities as the change in physical output, if not more so. In such cases, the use of real growth rates to indicate growth in consumption possibilities may involve a serious bias. It certainly does involve such a bias for the oil-exporting countries during 1950–75, and the bias is clearly in a downward direction.

will not even begin to reduce the absolute gap between them until
the ratio of their per capita incomes is equal to the inverse ratio of
their growth rates. For example, even though Korea has been
growing twice as fast as the OECD countries for the past fifteen
years, the absolute gap between them will continue to widen until
the per capita GNP of Korea reaches half that of the OECD countries. The proportion is currently not one-half but one-tenth.

Assuming for a moment that historical growth rates continue
into the future and ignoring the fact that cross-country comparisons of conventional GNP per capita statistics are misleading, it is
possible to calculate for each developing country the number of
years that it would take until the absolute gap between it and the
OECD countries would be closed (Table 9). For the large majority
of developing countries, containing most of the developing
world's population, the gap would never be closed, for their
measured rate of growth of per capita GNP has historically been
slower than that of the OECD countries. Even among the fastest-
growing developing countries, only eight would close the gap
within 100 years, and only sixteen would close it within 1,000
years.[14]

Welfare implications of the gaps

It is not clear that "narrowing the relative gap" makes much
sense as a development objective. To take a simple example, if
the per capita income of Bangladesh as conventionally measured
rises by $2 while that of the United States rises by $65, the relative gap would be narrowing—yet this hardly seems like a shining

14. These time intervals may be quite different if purchasing-power
parity GNP estimates are used, though the direction and magnitude of this
difference will not be clear until it is established how growth rates calculated using purchasing-power parities differ from those rates calculated
using conventional GNP statistics: see Bhagwati and Hansen [1972],
Kravis, Heston, and Summers [1977 and 1977a], and Strout [1977]. For
an alternative formulation in which the gap is measured as the number
of decades by which specific developing countries lag behind developed
countries, see Chenery [1976].

Table 9. The Absolute Gap: When Might It Be Closed? [a]

Country [b]	GNP per capita, 1975 (1974 U.S. dollars)	Annual growth rate, 1960–75 (percent)	Number of years until gap closed if 1960–75 growth rates continue
OECD countries	5,238	3.7	—
Libyan Arab Republic	4,675	11.8	2
Saudi Arabia	2,767	8.6	14
Singapore	2,307	7.6	22
Israel	3,287	5.0	37
Iran	1,321	6.9	45
Hong Kong	1,584	6.3	48
Korea	504	7.3	69
China (Taiwan)	817	6.3	75
Iraq	1,180	4.4	223
Brazil	927	4.2	362
Thailand	319	4.5	365
Tunisia	695	4.2	422
Syrian Arab Republic	604	4.2	451
Lesotho	161	4.5	454
Turkey	793	4.0	675
Togo	245	4.1	807
Panama	977	3.8	1,866
Malawi	137	3.9	1,920
Malaysia	665	3.8	2,293
Papua New Guinea	412	3.8	2,826
China, People's Republic of	320	3.8	2,900
Mauritania	288	3.8	3,224

a. Absolute gap is GNP per capita of the OECD countries ($2,378 in 1950, $5,238 in 1975) less GNP per capita of the individual country.

b. All developing countries with population of 1 million or more whose growth rate of per capita income exceeded that of the OECD countries during 1960–75.

Source: Computed from data tapes, *World Bank Atlas* (1977).

goal worth striving toward.[15] "Narrowing the absolute gap" appears to make more intuitive sense in welfare terms. But since it may take centuries before the absolute gap is narrowed—if

15. In fact, each year's increase in measured GNP per capita in the United States is currently equal to about a century's increase in Bangladesh or India. This is more than a little misleading, however, since a 1 or 2 percent increase in per capita income probably does more to increase economic welfare in Bangladesh than a similar percentage increase does in the United States.

it is ever narrowed—in most developing countries, to use this as a central goal of development is to guarantee long-term frustration.[16]

Fortunately, there are compelling reasons to believe that most developing countries will not place the closing of the gap at the center of their aspirations. First, not all of them regard the resource-wasting life style of the developed countries as an end toward which it is worth striving; at least some seem to prefer to create their own development patterns based on their own resources, and needs, and traditions.[17]

Second, when thinking of the per capita income that they would like to attain, most people (and governments) tend to think of the income of a close-by reference group. Thus, for example, despite the fact that within most countries there is a clear positive association between income and self-rated happiness, there is no observable tendency for people in poor countries to rate themselves as less happy on average than people in rich countries rate themselves [Easterlin 1974]. There are several possible explanations of this apparent paradox [Abramovitz 1975]. One of them is simply that most people in poor countries do not regard the rich foreigners as part of their reference group and hence are not overconcerned with the gap. They are more concerned, it seems with their own internal income distributions and their own place within them.[18]

16. The 1974 U.N. General Assembly resolution on the New International Economic Order and the Leontief model [United Nations 1976], both place primary importance on reduction of the gap. Compare Lewis's concluding remarks to a special conference on the gap: "What will happen to the gap between the rich and the poor countries? . . . I do not know the answer and . . . since I think what matters is the absolute progress of the LDCs and not the size of the gap, I do not care" [1972, p. 420].

17. Compare Haq [1976, p. 2]: "The concept of catching up must be rejected. Catching up with what? Surely the Third World does not wish to imitate the life styles of the rich nations? It must meet its own basic human needs within the framework of its own cultural values, building development around people rather than people around development."

18. The multicountry study by Cantril [1965] indicates that the elite in developing countries tend to be more concerned with the international gap than poorer people. For some empirical evidence on the income distribution and self-rated happiness, see Morawetz and others [1977].

3

The Reduction of Poverty

*There is, perhaps, no better test of the
progress of a nation than that which
shows what proportion are in poverty.*

BOWLEY [*1923, p. 214*]

ONE OF THE PRINCIPAL PROBLEMS WITH USING GROWTH in average per capita income as the sole index of development is that it grants equal importance to each extra dollar of income, regardless of whether that dollar is earned by a rich or a poor person. Ideally, of course, it would be desirable to measure growth in weighted per capita income, with each extra dollar being multiplied by the social welfare weight attached to its recipient. The welfare weights would presumably be heavier for the poor than for the rich and might also vary by location, occupation, or other criteria. Unfortunately, since there is seldom agreement on the precise welfare weights to be applied to different income recipients, the ideal cannot usually be calculated in practice. For this reason, interest has recently returned to various second-best, partial indicators of welfare, which may be used in conjunction with data on average per capita income to examine the extent to which growth has improved the economic condition of the poor. Among these supplementary indicators, some relate to employment, others are concerned with the income distribution, and a third set relates to fulfillment of basic needs. These will be discussed in turn, with particular reference in each case to the relationship (if any) between the rate of growth of income per capita and performance on the particular indicator.

Employment

Conventional wisdom has it that unemployment has been increasing over time in many, if not most, developing countries.[1] This claim is usually based not on hard data, but on the twin observations (a) that there seem to be increasing numbers of unemployed persons in the cities and (b) that because of rapid population growth, the labor force is increasing at a faster rate than employment opportunities in the formal sector.[2]

Before examining this claim, consider for a moment the nature of unemployment in developing countries. Most people in such countries work in family or self-employment in agriculture, services, and informal industry, in which the notion of a "job" is much less clear than in the formal sector. Furthermore, in the absence of unemployment compensation, only the relatively well-off can afford to be openly unemployed. Therefore, in most developing countries the employment problem expresses itself more as underemployment—working too few hours or with excessively low productivity—than as open unemployment.

What has been happening to rates of underemployment in developing countries over time? Nobody really knows, and, what is more, it may not be possible to know. A detailed study of almost any group in the informal sector of a developing country indicates the nature of the problem. Take, for example, the small traders, freight carriers, shoeshiners, and newspaper sellers in the town of Castro in southern Chile.[3] Currently, most of these people

---

1. See, for example, the references cited by Ramos [1974, n. 1].

2. On the causes of the generally poor, but occasionally successful, performance of formal industry in absorbing labor, see, for example, Bruton [1973], Edwards [1974], Morawetz [1974], Ranis [1975], and Lydall [1977a].

3. Morawetz [1978]. On informal sector underemployment, see also Berry [1972], Mazumdar [1975], and a number of informal sector studies done under the ILO's World Employment Program: for example, Joshi, Lubell, and Mouly [1976], and Kritz and Ramos [1976].

spend long hours each day waiting for raw materials or customers, during which time their productivity is literally zero. They say that they are more underemployed now than they were in the boom times of a few years ago. But there is no way of verifying such a claim, for it would be necessary to spend weeks observing and interviewing various groups of such informal sector families at different dates to get a feeling for change in their degree of underemployment. And at the end of it all, it is most unlikely that an "underemployment percentage" could be estimated that would have any meaning in either a time series or a cross-section context. Their real income would probably be the best proxy for their real level of employment, but it, too, would be difficult to estimate.

The only historical data that are available on unemployment or underemployment are figures on open unemployment in a small number of countries for the period between 1960 and 1974. These data are deficient for two principal reasons. They do not measure the concept that is needed, which is unemployment *plus* underemployment. And even what they do measure, they do not always measure accurately or consistently. For example, labor force surveys often place urban open unemployment in India at around 3 percent. But after making a series of simple and apparently quite reasonable adjustments, Turnham [1971] concludes that the true rate may be closer to 6 to 9 percent.[1]

Bearing in mind these two serious problems, the historical evidence that is available on open unemployment is summarized in Table 10. The data cover nine countries in Latin America, three nations in East Asia, and one country each in Africa and the Middle East. In most of these countries open unemployment seems to have fluctuated around a fairly constant trend, whereas in Korea and Taiwan it clearly declined.[5] But note that no histori-

4. Other, even more cautionary examples have also been documented. The first volume of the 1971 census in Indonesia put the unemployment rate at 2.2 percent, whereas a later volume of the same census put it at 8.9 percent. The difference is apparently explained by the classification of doubtful cases of inconsistent coding as "employed" in the first volume, but as "unemployed" in the later one [Arndt 1975].

5. Keesing [1977] finds that Mexican unemployment rates in the 1930s and 1940s were as high as, and maybe higher than, they are today.

Table 10. Open Unemployment Rates, Selected Countries, by Year, 1960–74

Country	Average percentage of open unemployment														
	1960	1961	1962	1963	1964	1965	1966	1967	1968	1969	1970	1971	1972	1973	1974
Africa															
Egypt, Arab Republic of	4.8	3.2	1.8	n.a.	1.9	n.a.	n.a.	n.a.	3.1	2.7	2.4	1.5	n.a.	n.a.	n.a.
Asia															
China (Taiwan)	n.a.	n.a.	n.a.	n.a.	4.4	3.4	3.1	2.3	1.7	1.9	1.7	1.7	1.5	n.a.	n.a.
Korea	n.a.	n.a.	8.4	8.1	7.7	7.4	7.1	6.2	5.1	4.8	4.5	4.5	4.5	4.0	5.4
Philippines	6.3	7.5	8.0	6.3	6.4	8.2	7.2	8.2	7.8	6.7	n.a.	4.8	6.9	4.4	n.a.
Middle East															
Syrian Arab Republic	n.a.	8.5	6.0	10.6	11.4	7.4	5.5	5.3	7.4	4.3	6.4	7.5	4.7	4.5	n.a.

Latin America

Argentina (Buenos Aires)	n.a.	n.a.	n.a.	n.a.	5.7	5.3	5.6	6.4	5.0	4.3	4.8	6.0	6.6	6.1	n.a.
Bolivia	n.a.	n.a.	n.a.	n.a.	n.a.	n.a.	n.a.	n.a.	n.a.	n.a.	15.9	16.1	16.3	16.4	16.1
Chile (Gran Santiago)	7.4	6.7	5.3	5.1	5.3	5.4	5.4	6.1	6.1	6.2	7.2	5.5	4.8	4.4	9.7
Colombia (Bogotá)	n.a.	n.a.	n.a.	7.9	7.1	8.9	10.1	12.2	11.5	9.6	8.2	8.9	6.8	n.a.	10.0
Panama	n.a.	n.a.	n.a.	5.8	7.4	7.6	5.1	6.2	7.0	6.6	7.1	7.6	6.8	6.5	n.a.
Peru (Lima-Callao)	n.a.	n.a.	n.a.	n.a.	n.a.	n.a.	n.a.	n.a.	7.0	7.0	7.0	n.a.	n.a.	7.7	6.5
Trinidad and Tobago	n.a.	n.a.	n.a.	n.a.	n.a.	14.0	14.0	15.0	15.0	13.5	12.5	12.6	n.a.	14.0	n.a.
Uruguay (Montevideo)	n.a.	n.a.	n.a.	n.a.	n.a.	n.a.	n.a.	n.a.	8.4	8.7	7.5	7.6	7.7	8.9	n.a.
Venezuela (urban)	n.a.	n.a.	n.a.	n.a.	n.a.	n.a.	n.a.	7.7	6.3	6.5	6.3	6.0	n.a.	n.a.	n.a.

Note: Since different definitions of unemployment are applied by various countries, the figures do not provide a consistent basis of comparison. At best, they can only give a rough indication of the direction of change in open unemployment over time—if it can be assumed that the definition used by each country remains relatively constant over time.

n.a. Not available.

Source: World Bank, "Urban Poverty and Employment," Draft Issues Paper, 1976 (processed), based on: *ILO Yearbook of Labor Statistics, 1968, 1972, 1974*, Table 10 unless otherwise indicated. Colombia, CEDE, Universidad de los Andes. Peru, Ministerio del Trabajo, Direccion General del Empleo, *Situación ocupacional del Peru*, 1974. Bolivia, World Bank, *Current Economic Position and Prospects of Bolivia*, Report 786a-30, Table 1.6. Taiwan, Taiwan Provincial Labor Force Survey and Research Institute, *Quarterly Report on the Labor Force Survey in Taiwan*, Republic of China, no. 37.

cal data are available for the poor, populous South Asian countries, and that nothing at all can be said with certainty about the trend in underemployment.

Some characteristics of open unemployment seem to be common throughout the developing countries.[6] The rate of open unemployment tends to be higher for the urban labor force than for the rural (Table 11); higher for men than for women; and particularly high among the youngest members of the labor force, who account for the largest percentage of total open unemployment. Among young people, those with higher levels of education and greatest means of family support tend to exhibit the highest rate of unemployment. Joblessness among such people is presumably less of a social problem than would be similar rates among heads of households.

In summary, since rates of underemployment cannot be measured with any degree of certainty, it is not possible to determine the degree of success that has been achieved over time in tackling the unemployment problem in developing countries. Nevertheless, in most of the countries for which partial, unsatisfactory evidence is available, the situation at least may not have worsened since 1960.[7] If this is the case, why do so many observers seem convinced that unemployment has increased? First, there may be a simple confusion between absolute numbers and percentages; when population is growing, even if the number of unemployed persons increases, the unemployment rate may still be constant or falling.[8] Second, it may be that the unemployment problem is not so new as is the increased awareness of it.

6. This paragraph is based on World Bank [1976].

7. Compare Turnham [1971, p. 136]: "The available data . . . show constancy in rates rather than any general tendency for rates to increase; in some countries rates have gone up but in others rates have come down. . . . We do not wish to de-emphasize the importance of the open unemployment problem but rather to suggest that the facts and the absence of facts should be given due weight in statements which essentially relate to quantities. . . . [S]omewhere on the way the importance of finding out what is really happening seems somehow to get lost."

8. In response, it might well be argued that the trend in absolute number of unemployed persons is of more interest than the trend in the percentage rate of unemployment.

Table 11. Open Unemployment Rates, Selected Countries, Specific Years, 1967–75

		Open unemployment rate (percent)	
Country	Year	Urban	Total
Africa			
Egypt, Arab Republic of	1971	n.a.	1.5
Ghana	1970	n.a.	6.0
Tanzania	1971	n.a.	10.0
Average, Africa [a]	1975	10.8	7.1
Asia			
China (Taiwan)	1972	n.a.	1.5
India	1971	n.a.	3.9
Indonesia	1971	4.8	2.2
Korea	1974	n.a.	5.4
Malaysia	1967/68	9.9	6.8
Pakistan	1972	n.a.	2.0
Philippines	1971	11.0	5.3
Sri Lanka	1969/70	16.9	13.2
Thailand	1969	1.3	0.2
Turkey	1969	4.9	n.a.
Average, Asia [a, b]	1975	6.9	3.9
Middle East			
Syrian Arab Republic	1973	n.a.	4.5
Latin America			
Bolivia	1974	n.a.	9.7
Brazil	1970	n.a.	2.0–2.4
Colombia	1974	10.0	n.a.
El Salvador	1975	4.9–8.6	5.2
Honduras	1972	n.a.	8.0
Mexico	1970	n.a.	3.7
Panama	1973	n.a.	6.5
Peru	1974	6.5	n.a.
Trinidad and Tobago	1973	n.a.	14.0
Uruguay	1973	8.9	n.a.
Venezuela	1971	6.0	n.a.
Average, Latin America [a]	1975	6.5	5.1

n.a. Not available.

a. ILO estimate.

b. Excluding the People's Republic of China and other Asian countries with centrally planned economies.

Source: World Bank, "Urban Poverty and Employment," Draft Issues Paper, 1976 (processed), based on *ILO Yearbook of Labor Statistics* (various years); country census and labor force survey statistics; World Bank country economic reports.

Incomes of the Poor

To increase employment is not an objective in itself; rather, what is wanted is to raise the incomes of the poor both absolutely and relative to the incomes of the rich. What has happened to the incomes of the poorest people in developing countries during the past twenty-five years?

Relative poverty

> *It may not be an exaggeration to say that we deal here not with* data *on the distribution of income by size but with estimates or judgments by courageous and ingenious scholars.*
>
> KUZNETS [*1963, p. 12*]

On certain simplifying assumptions, the degree of relative poverty in a society may be measured by the degree of inequality of the income distribution.[9] From cross-section evidence it seems

9. This section is based on empirical work and partial or comprehensive surveys by Adelman and her associates [1973, 1975a, 1976, and 1977], Paukert [1973], Ahluwalia [1974, 1976, and 1977], Chenery and others [1974], Srinivasan and Bardhan [1974], Cline [1975], Papanek [1975], Berry and Urrutia [1976], Fei, Ranis, and Kuo [1976], Felix [1976], Foxley [1976], Griffin [1976], Jolly [1976], Lal [1976], Musgrove [1976], Renaud [1976], Weisskoff and Figueroa [1976], Ahluwalia and Duloy [1977], Bacha [1977], Griffin [1977], Griffin and Khan [1977 and 1977a], Lipton [1977], Lydall [1977], Pyatt [1977], Rao [1978], Warren [1977], Webb [1977], and Westphal [1977]. Since the first printing of this book, Fei, Ranis, and Kuo [1977] has been scheduled for 1979 publication under the same title by Oxford University Press, and Westphal [1977] appeared as "The Republic of Korea's Experience with Export-Led Industrial Development" in *World Development,* vol. 6, no. 3 (1978), pp. 347–82.

that income inequality[10] increases in the early stages of development, but then begins to diminish after a per capita income of from $500 to $1,000 is reachèd (Table 12.)[11] But cross-section findings are influenced not only by natural forces, but also by the policies (such as import-substituting industrialization) pursued by particular countries or groups of countries during different periods. Thus, even if cross-section studies indicate that income inequality normally increases during the early stages of the development process, a country that follows policies different from those pursued by most nations in the past (or that has different insitutions or a different population structure) may be able to avoid or at least partly neutralize this stage.[12] In fact, the only way of knowing what has actually been happening to the share of the poorest people in developing countries over time is to examine directly the historical evidence for particular countries.[13]

Bearing in mind that historical data on income distribution are at least as problematical as cross-section figures, and often more so, what do the data show? In quite a large number of countries the share of the poorest people in GNP seems to have either increased or at least remained fairly constant over time. This group includes fast-growing, market-oriented countries such as Iran, Israel, Korea, Singapore, and Taiwan, as well as countries that have consciously concerned themselves with income distribution such as China. It also includes Costa Rica, El Salvador, and possibly Colombia and Puerto Rico. By contrast, in a second, also quite large group of countries, including Argentina, Brazil, Mexico,

10. On the different measures of inequality and some related problems, see, for example, Sen [1973], Atkinson [1975], Tinbergen [1975], Bruno [1977], Fields [1977], and Srinivasan [1977].
11. Kuznets [1955 and 1963] first suggested this inverted-U hypothesis. The most recent cross-section study is by Ahluwalia [1976]; see also Bacha [1977].
12. Ranis [1977] argues explicitly that Taiwan has managed to avoid the increasing-inequality stage as growth has taken place. For an interesting attempt to spell out the implications of the Kuznets curve for various partial indicators of poverty, see Ahluwalia and Duloy [1977].
13. Most cross-section investigators, including especially Ahluwalia [1976], are frank in recognizing these limitations to the approach.

Table 12. Cross-Section Estimates of Income Shares and Average Absolute Income Levels of Low-Income Groups, Developing Countries, Various Years

	Lowest 40 percent		Lowest 20 percent	
GNP per capita (U.S. dollars, 1971)	Income share (percent)	Absolute income (U.S. dollars, 1971)	Income share (percent)	Absolute income (U.S. dollars, 1971)
75	22.42	42.04	8.68	32.55
100	20.07	50.16	7.66	38.30
200	15.47	77.34	5.63	56.31
300	13.49	101.15	4.72	70.84
400	12.40	123.97	4.20	84.05
500	11.73	146.65	3.87	96.76
600	11.31	169.59	3.65	109.36
700	11.03	193.00	3.49	122.06
800	10.85	216.98	3.38	134.98
900	10.74	241.59	3.29	148.21
1,000	10.68	266.87	3.24	161.79
1,500	10.76	403.62	3.14	235.74
3,000	15.00	909.14	4.38	519.13

Note: These estimates are based on regression equations predicting the income shares of the lowest income groups as estimated from cross country data. These predicted income shares are based on the assumption that explanatory variables other than per capita GNP in the regression equation are held constant at their mean value for the sample. When per capita GNP is used as the sole explanatory variable, the income shares are somewhat lower for the earlier stages, and the turning point occurs at about $500. For details, see Ahluwalia (1976).

Source: Reproduced from Ahluwalia and Duloy (1976), appendix.

Panama, Peru, India, Malaysia, and Philippines, the share of the poorest people seems to have declined over time.

It is interesting that there seems to be no clear relationship between the rate of economic growth and either (a) the degree of inequality at a point in time or (b) the trend of inequality over time. Fast growers include both equal and unequal societies; they also include societies that have been growing more, and less, unequal. The same is true, also, of slow growers.

The available evidence on growth and distribution seems to suggest two working hypotheses. First, the initial distribution of assets and incomes may be a crucial determinant of the trend in inequality. People who already own assets, whether physical or human capital, are in the best position to profit once growth begins. Thus, a society that begins growing with an unequal income distribution is quite likely to remain unequal or become more so, whereas one in which initial disparities are small may be able to avoid a significant increase in inequality. Second, and not unrelated, both real-world and simulation evidence indicates that the most powerful determinant of the income distribution is the underlying structure of the economy. In other words, once growth is taking place and incomes are being earned, it seems to be difficult to redistribute income by means of taxes, public employment, and the like.[14]

Putting these two working hypotheses together (and at this stage they are no more than hypotheses) yields potentially powerful implications for policy. In particular, the historical evidence suggests that it simply may not be possible to "grow first and redistribute later," because the structure of growth may largely fix the pattern of distribution, at least until much higher developed-country levels of per capita income are approached. That is to say, if greater equality of incomes is to be an objective in the medium term, it may be necessary to tackle it as a first priority by land reform, mass education, and whatever other means are available, rather than leaving it until after growth has taken place.

14. See, for example, Meerman [1972], Bird and De Wulf [1973], Sen [1976], Adelman and Robinson [1977], Adelman and others [1977], Stewart [1977], and Taylor and Lysy [1977]; but compare Huang [1976].

Absolute poverty

Are there countries in which large numbers of the poorest people have experienced an absolute worsening of their economic situation over time? [15] Clearly, this cannot have been the case in nations in which the share of the poor in a growing GNP increased or remained constant. But what of countries in which the share of the poor declined?

Adelman and Morris argue on the basis of cross-section evidence that "development is accompanied by an absolute as well as a relative decline in the average income of the very poor" [1973, p. 189]. But this claim has been widely criticized as being an exaggerated inference, not warranted by the data on which it is based.[16] Further, after carrying out a separate, comprehensive cross-section study, Ahluwalia concludes in direct contradiction of Adelman and Morris that the results "do not support the stronger hypothesis . . . [of] prolonged absolute impoverishment of large sections of the population in the course of development" [1976, p. 338].

Although cross-section comparisons may be informative, it is necessary to turn again to time series data for particular countries to find out what has in fact happened. The data here are, if anything, even less reliable than those reported on in the previous section. The conclusions reached by different investigators often vary according to the data set used; occasionally, two researchers have drawn contrary inferences from a single set of evidence.

Among the most populous countries, only in China and pos-

---

15. The process of economic development is likely to lead to a deterioration in the absolute incomes of some socioeconomic groups because of the disruption of preexisting economic structures and marginalization of particular skills. The effects of the European enclosure movement and the decline of the Indian cotton industry in the face of competition from Lancashire are two often quoted examples. But the groups so displaced will not necessarily be among the poorest people, so that this general point is not sufficient to suggest that the poor must necessarily suffer in absolute terms from development [Ahluwalia and Duloy 1976].

16. See, for example, Cline [1976], Papanek [1975], Ahluwalia [1976], Ahluwalia and Duloy [1976], Lal [1976], and Little [1976]; and a reply by Adelman and Morris [1975].

sibly in Mexico does it seem to be agreed that there has been no large-scale absolute impoverishment among the poor. In Bangladesh, Brazil, India, Indonesia, and Pakistan the matter is in dispute.[17]

The weight of the evidence on impoverishment of the poor depends upon the way in which the disputed cases are read. If large numbers of the poorest people in South Asia, Brazil, and Indonesia have indeed become worse off over time, the balance may be quite black. Even if this is the case, however, the blame can hardly be laid at the door of "economic growth," for the list of countries in which some groups may have experienced absolute impoverishment includes at least as many slow growers as fast ones. Indeed, in countries such as Pakistan, Bangladesh, India, and Indonesia only sustained and equitably distributed economic growth will make any sort of dent in their massive poverty in the foreseeable future.

In setting priorities for future research, is it really important to clarify what has happened to absolute poverty in the past? There are strong arguments on both sides of the question. On the one hand, today's stylized facts of development go into tomorrow's models and policy formation, so they had better be right. On the other hand, given the problems with the historical data, it may simply prove impossible to resolve the question satisfactorily now or in the future. The debate on the fate of the English poor during the early stages of the industrial revolution dragged on inconclusively not just for decades but for more than a century.[18]

17. In addition, the poor seem to have become no worse off in Panama and Peru [Ahluwalia 1974], but there may have been some deterioration in Malaysia and Philippines [Griffin and Khan 1977 and 1977a]. On Brazil, see Fishlow [1972, 1973, and 1977], Langoni [1973], Bacha [1976], Tyler [1976], Bacha and Taylor [1977], and Lysy and Taylor [1977]; on India, Srinivasan and Bardhan [1974], Kumar [1974], Lal [1976], Ahluwalia [1977], and Griffin and Khan [1977]; on Indonesia, Arndt [1975], Gupta [1975], and Penny and McGee [1975]; on Mexico, Ahluwalia [1974]; and on Pakistan and Bangladesh, Guisinger and Irfan [1974], Griffin and Khan [1977 and 1977a], Guisinger [1977], and Naseem [1977].

18. See, for example, Hartwell and others [1972] and Adelman and Morris [1977].

Basic Needs

In the process of reducing poverty, even incomes are only a means to an end. The ultimate goal is provision to the poor of the goods and services required to fulfill their basic needs: food, health care, shelter, and the like.[19] The word "need" is defined by Webster's dictionary as "an urgent requirement of something essential or desirable that is lacking." Because "urgent requirement," "essential," and "desirable" are all subjective concepts, so too is "basic needs." In working with basic needs there are problems of precise definition and of variation of needs according to the climate, culture, and income level of the country concerned. Outsiders and local people sometimes rank needs quite differently.[20] This may stir up the ages-old question: should the poor get what they want or what some external authority believes that they need? With some indexes of basic needs there is a distribution problem similar to the one inherent in using statistics on average GNP per capita as a measure of welfare. Always, there is a weighting problem: which is to be preferred, a 10 percent increase in literacy and complete freedom from malaria or a 60 percent increase in literacy and no improvement in health?

None of this is meant to suggest that fulfilling the basic needs of the poorest people should not be one of the centerpoints of development strategies in developing countries. Rather, it is meant simply to illustrate that "basic needs" can be quite difficult to define and rank in practice, perhaps more so than it appeared when use of the concept was first suggested.

Nutrition

What has happened to standards of nutrition in developing countries in the past twenty-five years? Nobody really knows

19. On the concept of basic needs, its measurement, and some implications for development strategies, see Pant [1962], UNRISD [1966 and 1970], Haq [1971, 1976a, and 1977], Baster [1972], United Nations [1975], Grant [1976], Herrera and others [1976], ILO [1976, 1976a, and 1977], Jolly [1976], Khan [1976], Norbye [1976], Stewart and Streeten [1976], Burki and Voorhoeve [1977], Morawetz [1978], Richards [1977], Srinivasan [1977], Streeten [1977, 1977b], and Warren [1977].

20. For some concrete examples in the Chilean context, see Morawetz [1978].

exactly what the poor people in developing countries eat today, let alone what they ate twenty-five years ago.[21] In addition, there is considerable controversy over the concept of minimum daily food requirements. Is it sufficient to look only at calories and proteins, or do vitamins and minerals have to be considered as well? In either case, what is the appropriate minimum requirement? Most data on food consumption are regional or country averages. But like income, food is unequally distributed in developing countries. Any serious estimate of the numbers of malnourished people has to take this complication into account.[22]

Two recent studies that tackle these problems as well as the available data allow are Reutlinger and Selowsky [1976] and International Food Policy Research Institute [1977]. They conclude that the absolute number of persons with inadequate food intake has almost certainly increased since 1960, but that it is not clear whether the proportion of total population in the developing world suffering from undernutrition has been increasing, decreasing, or constant over time.[23]

Between 1961–65 and 1974, per capita calorie availability seems to have increased in forty-seven of fifty-seven FAO countries, and it no doubt increased in China as well. In heavily populated India, however, availability appears to have declined somewhat, while in seventeen of the forty-seven countries the increase for the full period is estimated to have been less than 5 percent. The regional distribution of the change in calorie availa-

21. For an introduction to the growing literature on nutrition, see the following works, several of which contain extensive bibliographies: Berg [1973], Joy [1973], Selowsky and Taylor [1973], World Bank [1973], Oftedal and Levinson [1974], United Nations [1974], Taylor [1975], Johnson [1976], Lappé and Collins [1976], Reutlinger and Selowsky [1976], Sarris and Taylor [1976], Sinha [1976], Timmer [1976], Wortman and others [1976], and International Food Policy Research Institute (hereinafter IFPRI) [1977].

22. Thus, a developing country with a typical, relatively unequal income distribution probably needs to reach at least 110 percent of average per capita calorie and protein requirements before most of its poor attain the minimum required protein-energy supply.

23. Data on trends in fulfillment of per capita calorie requirements vary significantly according to the source, and even data from the same source sometimes change substantially from year to year as figures are revised.

bility was significantly skewed: Latin America, North Africa, and the Middle East showed substantial gains; in Asia, excluding China, availability was on balance constant; while in sub-Saharan Africa the situation deteriorated. Per capita protein availability generally increased a few percentage points less (or decreased a few points more) than per capita calorie availability, which indicates an apparent average tendency toward regression in the quality of the diet.

One not easily quantifiable element must be added to this discussion of trends in nutrition. In cases of severe food crisis or famine, it is less likely today than it was twenty-five years ago that large numbers of people would starve to death. Communications have improved, awareness of need is greater, and emergency food aid is more readily available.

How serious is the undernutrition problem in absolute terms? In a well-known aggregative study that ignores the intracountry income distribution problem, the FAO estimated that more than 460 million people had an insufficient protein-energy supply in 1970 [FAO 1975]. By contrast, Reutlinger and Selowsky [1976], using a method that takes distribution explicitly into account, estimate that from 0.9 to 1.1 billion people received less than the recommended daily calorie intake in 1965, and that this figure was likely to have increased to from 1.1 to 1.4 billion by 1975.[24] The higher order of magnitude of the Reutlinger-Selowsky estimates is due partly to their incorporation of the distribution factor; a second cause is that they use a slightly higher level of minimum requirements than the FAO. When Reutlinger and Selowsky adopt an alternative, lower definition of undernutrition (calorie deficit greater than 250 calories a day), the number of persons involved drops significantly, to from 0.4 to 0.9 billion, depending on the subsidiary assumptions.

It has been estimated that elimination of the 1975 calorie deficit would require increasing developing country food consumption by the equivalent of about 25–30 million tons of foodgrains [World Bank 1977].[25] This represents about 2 percent of current

24. A subsequent calculation by IFPRI [1977], which uses a similar methodology and more recent data, arrives at similar orders of magnitude.
25. Using different assumptions, IFPRI [1977] reaches an order of magnitude twice as great.

world production of grains, or close to 100 percent of the grain imports of the deficit countries concerned. But this is only one blade of the scissors. The nutrition problem in developing countries is not simply one of insufficient production of food. Just as critical is the question: how can the increased production be got into the hands of the people who are undernourished? Partly, this is an income problem: if the poor had more money with which to buy food, the undernutrition problem would be more than half solved.[26] But distribution considerations are important too. In particular, when large developing countries import food, logistic and distribution problems often prevent distant and scattered rural communities from receiving their share. This suggests that, if the nutrition problem is to be solved at the mass level, it may be necessary for at least the largest developing countries to increase production themselves rather than relying on imports from the developed world.[27] A second strong argument working in the same direction is that food surpluses in the developed countries may not always be available when needed.

Health

> *Just about any junk-producing new*
> *import-substituting industry has had a*
> *bigger impact . . . [on developing*
> *country national accounts than] the*
> *decline in infant mortality.*
>
> DÍAZ-ALEJANDRO [*1975, p. 11*]

Most indexes of the general standard of a nation's health suffer from severe shortcomings. Mortality statistics do not take sufficient account of diseases that generally cause sickness rather than

26. An increase in demand where no increase in supply is forthcoming may, however, cause prices to rise and the poorest people to be even more undernourished than before. Similarly, a large exogenous increase in supply that is not accompanied by an increase in demand may cause grain prices to fall, creating hardship among the many small farmers.
27. In large countries such as India this argument may also apply to particular regions. On the experience of the Indian state of Kerala, see United Nations [1975].

Table 13. Life Expectancy at Birth, by Region, 1935–39, 1950–55, and 1965–70
(Years)

Region	1935–39	1950–55	1965–70
South Asia	30	41	49
East Asia	30	45	52
Africa	30	36	43
Latin America	40	52	60
China, People's Republic of	n.a.	48	60
Developing countries	32	42	49
Developed countries	56	65	70

n.a. Not available.
Source: World Bank (1974), Annex Table 2. China data from United Nations (1975a), p. 99.

death nor of the age structure of the population. Data on the number of doctors or nurses per thousand people do not allow for differences in length and usefulness of training, nor for the regional distribution of such personnel; in some countries almost all may be concentrated in a few cities, while in others they may be scattered throughout the countryside.[28]

When all the problems are taken into account, national life expectancy at various ages is probably the best single indicator of national health levels. In the past couple of decades the developing countries have registered increases in life expectancy that took a century to achieve in the industrialized countries. Today, life expectancy stands at fifty years, a level attained in western Europe only at the beginning of this century (Table 13).[29] The increases reflect primarily a sharp drop in infant mortality rates and provide one of the strongest available indications that since 1950 real standards of living have risen on a broad front in the

28. For more detail on these and other problems, see Sharpston [1972, c1975, and n.d.] and World Bank [1975].
29. This average figure for life expectancy masks considerable regional diversity. Expectancy ranges from sixty years in Latin America and China to forty-three years in Africa.

developing world, because the increases in life expectancy were more the result of general improvements in living conditions than more closely defined medical improvements. There was also considerable progress in the latter sphere, however, especially in control of communicable diseases. By 1975 plague (which claimed more than 10 million lives in developing countries during the first 20 years of the twentieth century) and smallpox had been virtually eradicated; while malaria (which seemed to have been eliminated by 1966 but subsequently rebounded) and cholera undoubtedly kill fewer people today than they did in 1950.[30]

In health care many developing countries have followed the model of the industrialized countries which is based on expensively trained medical personnel and curative medicine. A steadily increasing number, however, have taken the alternative route of teaching minimal skills to large numbers of paramedical personnel and concentrating on social and preventive rather than private and curative medicine, in rural as well as urban areas. The most famous example, of course, is China, where health levels appear now to be roughly equivalent to those of the United States in the 1930s—a remarkable achievement for a country with a per capita income of not much more than $300.[31]

Despite these improvements in health levels in developing countries, significant problems remain. Perhaps the most serious one—though even here improvements have been registered—is the generally low level of sanitation, which may be seen in the large numbers of people (close to half the population of the developing world) who do not have adequate access to a safe water supply and sewerage disposal (Table 14).[32]

30. No systematic data are available on the large number of nonfatal but often debilitating diseases commonly found in developing countries.

31. Sharpston [c1975].

32. For a detailed study of the availability of rural water supply in developing countries, see Saunders and Warford [1976].

Table 14. Relation between Access to Water Supply and Sewerage and per Capita Income, Developing Countries, c1970

	Per capita income, 1970 (U.S. dollars)			
Item	Less than 100	101 to 150	151 to 450	More than 450
Number of countries	15	17	34	12
Percentage of population with access to water supply				
Rural, with reasonable access	13	8 [a]	28	32
Urban, with public standpost	24	31	21	17
Urban, with pipe to house	21	36	58	63
Percentage of population with access to sewage disposal				
Rural, adequate	7	12	26	n.a.
Urban, other disposal methods [b]	54	67	40	n.a.
Urban, sewage system	6	14	24	n.a.

Note: These estimates were obtained by calculating the population-weighted average of reported coverage within the group of countries. The definitions of coverage and of urban and rural are those developed by the individual countries and hence are not comparable. Furthermore, no attempt has been made to evaluate the quality of these statistics at the country level. The values reported in this table should therefore be interpreted only as crude "order of magnitude" indicators.

n.a. Not available.

a. This value is dominated by India and Pakistan, which report 6 percent and 3 percent access, respectively.

b. Buckets, pit privies, and septic tanks not connected to a public sewer system.

Source: World Bank (1975), Table 6, based on WHO statistics.

Housing

> *A house may be large or small: as long as the surrounding houses are equally small it satisfies all social demands for a dwelling. But let a palace arise beside the little house, and it shrinks from a little house to a hut.*
>
> KARL MARX [*quoted by Griffin 1976, p. 11*]

Not only are needs for housing, or "shelter," relative in Marx's sense, they also vary significantly according to climate. To blur the picture further, the most commonly used data on housing—

estimates of the number of persons per room—do not specify the size of the room nor the materials of which it is constructed.

Deficient as they are, the time series data that are available on housing indicate that in a number of countries the average number of persons per room declined between 1960 and 1970, and that some progress was also made in bringing piped water and electricity to dwellings (Table 15). It should be noted, however, that most of the countries for which evidence is available are in Latin America. Africa is hardly represented at all, and the only evidence for the South Asia region, that for number of persons per dwelling in India, shows a deterioration.

Perhaps the most urgent need in the housing field, especially in urban areas, is to provide low-cost, possibly self-help housing at prices that the majority of the poor can afford. A recent detailed

Table 15. Housing Indicators, Selected Countries, 1960 and 1970

Country	Average number of persons per room		Dwellings with piped water (percent of total)		Dwellings with electricity (percent of total)	
	1960	1970	1960	1970	1960	1970
Africa						
Morocco	2.2	2.4 [a]	n.a.	n.a.	77	82
South Asia						
India	2.6	2.8 [a]	n.a.	n.a.	n.a.	n.a.
East Asia						
Korea, Republic of	2.5	2.3	21	38	28	50
Latin America						
Argentina	1.4	1.4	n.a.	n.a.	n.a.	n.a.
Brazil	n.a.	n.a.	21	39	39	48
Chile	1.6	1.4	56	78	n.a.	n.a.
Costa Rica	1.5	1.3	n.a.	n.a.	n.a.	n.a.
Jamaica	n.a.	n.a.	37	38	n.a.	n.a.
Mexico	2.9	2.5	32	49	n.a.	n.a.
Nicaragua	2.8	2.9 [a]	n.a.	n.a.	n.a.	n.a.
Panama	2.4	2.2	46	64	44	52
Peru	2.2	2.3 [a]	n.a.	n.a.	30	32
Puerto Rico	n.a.	n.a.	70	77	n.a.	n.a.
Venezuela	n.a.	n.a.	67	73	78	77 [a]

Note: All three indicators are described as of "relatively good comparability" for 1960 and 1970. For tables that incorporate a slightly larger sample of countries but use somewhat different definitions, see World Bank, *World Tables 1976*, pp. 524–27.
  n.a. Not available.
  a. Figure denotes a deterioration in 1970 as compared with 1960.
Source: Warren (1977), Table 14, based on UNRISD data.

study finds that one-third to two-thirds of all families in Ahmed-abad, Bogotá, Hong Kong, Madras, Mexico City, and Nairobi cannot afford the cheapest new housing currently being built.[33]

Education

Between 1950 and 1970 the number of pupils in primary schools in developing countries trebled, reaching 200 million. During the same period the number of students in secondary and tertiary education increased sixfold, reaching 42 and 6 million, respectively, by 1970.[34] The increases in attendance rates are equally remarkable if viewed in percentage terms, and were widely shared throughout Africa, Asia, and Latin America (Table 16).

The proportion of adults in the developing countries who are literate, which stood at about one-third in 1950, had risen to over one-half by 1975. On a regional basis Latin American literacy rates rose from 65 percent in 1960 to 75 percent ten years later; Asian rates, from 45 to 53 percent; and African rates, from 20 to 26 percent.[35]

These crude indexes demonstrate indisputably that there have been significant increases in the quantity of education in develop-ing countries during the past couple of decades. But there is some disagreement over what has happened, and what ought to happen, with respect to quality. It has been argued, for example, that edu-cation in developing countries often has not been directed to the needs of the persons receiving it.[36] Education patterned on the academic model of the industrialized countries, the argument con-tinues, may have contributed to the disruptively high rates of

33. Grimes [1976]; see also World Bank [1975a].
34. World Bank [1974a], based on Unesco statistics.
35. World Bank [1974a], based on Unesco statistics.
36. Coombs and Ahmed [1974], Edwards and Todara [1974], and World Bank [1974a] present recent statements of this point of view. For discussions of three attempts that have been made to tailor education to national neeeds, see Carnoy and Wertheim [1976] on Cuba, Maliyamkono [1976] on Tanzania, and Tannebaum and Simmons [1977] on China; also Simmons [forthcoming].

Table 16. Percentage of Children Attending School, by Region, 1950, 1960, and 1970

Region	1950	1960	1970
Children aged 5–14 attending primary school			
Africa	17	28	n.a.
Asia	25	42	n.a.
Latin America	38	49	n.a.
Children of primary school age attending at any level			
Africa	n.a.	34	48
Asia	n.a.	50	59
Latin America	n.a.	60	78
Children of secondary school age attending at any level			
Africa	n.a.	12	25
Asia	n.a.	22	44
Latin America	n.a.	26	49

n.a. Not available.
Source: Warren (1977), Tables 10–12, based on United Nations, *Report on the World Social Situation* (New York: United Nations, 1963 and 1974).

rural-urban migration by making villagers dissatisfied with their lot, instead of providing them with skills relevant to their rural situation. Similarly, tertiary education has rarely been consciously tailored to meet national requirements; in a few notable cases, such as medicine in the Philippines, it seems to have served foreign needs as much as local ones by ensuring a continuing inexpensive supply of trained personnel who migrate to the industrialized countries.[37]

Yet although governments have been proposing for up to 100 years that education ought to be tailored to local needs,[38] it seems to be difficult in practice to implement these suggestions satisfactorily. Where locally oriented education has been introduced, one of its main effects has often been simply to lower the quality of the instruction provided. This harms the individual receiving the education by limiting possibilities for personal development and eco-

37. Bhagwati [1976] and Bhagwati and Partington [1976].
38. In Ghana (earlier West Africa and the Gold Coast) this subject was stressed in every major education report from 1842 until independence in 1957 [Foster 1965].

nomic advancement;[39] it may also damage the country's prospects for keeping up with or contributing to important (and posssibly relevant) developments in science and technology. What is more, low-quality education, once installed, tends to repeat itself generation after generation.

Both of the points of view embodied in the previous two paragraphs have some appealing aspects; it is not clear exactly where the balance lies between them.

Basic needs and growth

Is it worth spending a lot of time and effort collecting and analyzing data on basic needs and devising strategies to fulfill them? Or would it be just as effective to concentrate solely on raising GNP per capita and leave the basic needs to take care of themselves? There are really two separate but related questions here. First, at any given time is there a significant positive relationship across countries between performance on indexes of basic needs and GNP per capita? Second, holding constant the initial level of per capita GNP, is there a significant relationship between improvement on indexes of basic needs and growth in GNP per capita?

In an attempt to shed some light on these two questions, sixteen indexes of basic needs and their rate of improvement were regressed on GNP per capita in separate equations for 1960, 1970, and growth during 1960–70.[40] In each equation, the sample includes all developing countries for which data are available. The data are, of course, as problematical as ever.[41]

The results of the regressions are summarized in Table 17. In

39. Mexico, following John Dewey's model, experimented with the establishment of special rural schools in the 1920s and 1930s. After ten years or so rural areas demanded the same schooling as urban ones, so they would not be discriminated against and condemned to inferiority [Keesing 1975a].

40. No attempt is made here to investigate the underlying structure of any relationship that might exist.

41. Basic needs data are taken from the social indicators published in World Bank [1976a]. Countries excluded by Chenery and Syrquin [1975] in their study are also excluded here.

Table 17. Cross-Section Estimates of the Relation between GNP per Capita and Fulfillment of Basic Needs, 1960, 1970, and Growth during 1960–70

Dependent variable [a]	1960			1970			Growth, 1960–70			
	GNP per capita, 1960 (1)	$\bar{R}^2$ (2)	Number of observations (3)	GNP per capita, 1970 (4)	$\bar{R}^2$ (5)	Number of observations (6)	GNP per capita, 1960 (7)	Growth in GNP per capita, 1960–70 (8)	$\bar{R}^2$ (9)	Number of observations (10)
Nutrition										
Per capita calorie supply as percent of total requirements	0.05 (2.41)	0.06	62	0.05 (3.81)	0.16	66	−0.01 (−0.74)	0.17 (3.39)	0.17	62
Per capita protein supply (grams per day)	0.08 (2.03)	0.05	63	0.07 (2.56)	0.06	66	0.01 (0.20)	0.14 (2.71)	0.13	63
Per capita protein supply from animal or pulse (grams per day)	0.31 (3.51)	0.21	38	0.15 (2.59)	0.08	66	−0.01 (−0.26)	0.56 (3.68)	0.22	38
Health										
Infant mortality rate	−0.30 (−3.68)	0.29	41	−0.37 (−3.68)	0.29	46	−0.02 (−0.37)	−0.52 (−2.29)	0.10	29
Death rate at 1–4 years	−0.91 (−5.82)	0.66	20	−0.98 (−4.46)	0.48	20	−0.14 (−0.65)	−0.54 (−0.40)	−0.22	11
Life expectancy at birth	0.19 (4.63)	0.35	38	0.15 (7.62)	0.46	66	0.01 (0.24)	0.10 (1.27)	0.07	37

(Table continues on following page.)

55

Table 17 (continued)

Dependent variable [a]	1960			1970			Growth, 1960–70			
	GNP per capita, 1960 (1)	R^2 (2)	Number of observations (3)	GNP per capita, 1970 (4)	R^2 (5)	Number of observations (6)	GNP per capita, 1960 (7)	Growth in GNP per capita, 1960–70 (8)	R^2 (9)	Number of observations (10)
Health (continued)										
Population per doctor	−1.14 (−7.26)	0.49	52	−1.10 (−9.29)	0.57	66	0.05 (1.02)	−0.20 (−1.34)	−0.01	51
Population per nursing person	−0.43 (−3.26)	0.21	49	−0.49 (−4.74)	0.27	67	0.01 (0.14)	−0.19 (−0.57)	−0.01	49
Population per hospital bed	−0.56 (−5.27)	0.38	61	−0.46 (−5.15)	0.36	67	−0.01 (−0.17)	−0.02 (−0.15)	0.01	61
Housing										
Average number of persons per room	−0.15 (−2.67)	0.25	32	−0.08 (−0.85)	−0.12	22	−0.13 (−1.85)	0.30 (0.89)	0.17	10
Percent of dwellings without piped water	−0.01 (−0.07)	−0.11	27	−0.27 (−2.20)	0.15	21	−0.26 (−2.13)	−0.16 (−0.27)	0.42	8
Percent of dwellings with access to electricity	0.71 (2.64)	0.17	28	0.99 (4.33)	0.49	22	0.05 (0.75)	1.18 (3.57)	0.65	7

Education

Adult literacy rate	0.45 (2.47)	0.10	33	0.71 (7.02)	0.47	54	−0.14 (−1.75)	−0.08 (−0.18)	0.13	31
Primary school enrollment ratio	0.58 (5.50)	0.30	65	0.47 (6.70)	0.40	67	−0.08 (−1.70)	0.14 (0.91)	0.06	65
Secondary school enrollment ratio	0.97 (6.16)	0.37	65	0.77 (7.68)	0.48	67	−0.07 (−0.79)	0.01 (0.02)	−0.03	65
Vocational school enrollments as percent of secondary school enrollments	0.18 (1.11)	0.01	62	0.31 (2.08)	0.02	66	0.16 (1.22)	−0.12 (−0.25)	−0.03	61

Note: Figures in parentheses are *t*-statistics. All variables, dependent and explanatory, are in log form. The coefficient of a variable for countries' population was never significantly different from zero, and is not presented here. Following Chenery and Syrquin (1975), in regressions not presented here, the square of GNP per capita was added as an extra explanatory variable. It added little or nothing to the goodness of fit in most cases, however, whereas the high degree of collinearity between it and GNP per capita caused the significance level of both coefficients to be very low.

a. The dependent variables take on 1960 values for the first set of regressions (columns 1–3), 1970 values for the second set (columns 4–6), and growth 1960–70 for the third set (columns 7–10).

Sources: Data on basic needs: World Bank, *World Tables 1976*, Series IV, "Social Indicators." Data on GNP per capita: Data tapes, *World Bank Atlas* (1977).

1960 and 1970 there is a significantly positive, though on average weak, relationship between performance on the indexes of basic needs and the level of GNP per capita in almost all cases. But only on five of the sixteen indicators—three on nutrition, infant mortality, and percentage of dwellings with access to electricity—is there any significant relationship between improvement in fulfillment of basic needs over time (1960–70) and growth in per capita GNP. Furthermore, the strength of the correlation between indexes of basic needs and GNP per capita varies greatly according to the index and, for a given index, according to the time period.[42] The conclusion is that—at least as the concepts are usually measured, at least for a period as short as ten years, and if the data are believed—GNP per capita and its growth rate do not seem to provide satisfactory proxies for fulfillment of basic needs and improvements in the same.[43]

42. The highest correlations for a moment in time are for health indexes. For growth over time, none of the four sets shows uniformly high degrees of correlation.

43. For a more sanguine view of the possibilities of using per capita GNP as a proxy for basic needs, see Warren [1977], who bases his judgment on his reading of UNRISD [1966 and 1970]. See also McGranahan [1972] and Horvat [1974]. Note that the ranking of countries by basic needs indicators is often quite similar to that for GNP per capita [UNRISD 1966 and 1970; United Nations 1975b; World Bank 1975].

Sewell and ODC [1977] construct a "physical quality of life" (PQLI) index from an average of three indicators: life expectancy, infant mortality, and literacy. Their particular choice of indicators may be disputed—infant mortality and life expectancy tend to be highly positively correlated—as may the meaningfulness in general of attempts to construct such single-valued indexes. Nevertheless, the evidence presented here does support their claim that performance on the PQLI index is likely to differ significantly from that on GNP per capita. For a brief critique of the PQLI index see Ruderman [1977].

4

Self-Reliance and Economic Independence

IN ADDITION TO RAISING AVERAGE INCOME PER CAPITA and reducing poverty, many developing countries have had as an objective to increase national self-reliance and economic independence. As with the first two objectives, countries have differed widely in the degree of emphasis placed on this aim. Some, such as China, Burma, and Cuba, have given it high priority.

To date there seems to be no clear consensus about what "self-reliance" means.[1] Undoubtedly, it has not only economic but also

1. For discussions, most of them theoretical, of the notion of self-reliance, see Furtado [1963, 1967, and 1973], Johnson [1965], Green and Seidman [1968], Frank [1969, 1969a, and 1977], Sunkel [1969], Weisskopf [1972], Amin [1974, 1974a], Haq [1976a], Rothstein [1976], Stewart and Streeten [1976], Mansour [1977], Minhas [1977], Pugwash [1977], and Warren [1977]. For empirical work on the separate but not unrelated New International Economic Order, see, for example, the Leontief model [United Nations 1976] and the RIO report [Tinbergen 1976]. Much of the literature on self-reliance is written by authors writing outside the mainstream of development economics who present comprehensive ideological, sociocultural, and political critiques of the orthodox doctrines of development. Such writings have been underrepresented in this study; for an introduction to them, in addition to some of the references cited earlier in

59

political and psychological connotations. In economics, it does not usually mean autarky, or a totally self-sufficient national economy, except perhaps in the case of such a large resource-abundant country as China. It does usually include control of the economy in national hands, diversification of foreign ties and trade to reduce dependence on a single country or product, and reduced dependence on foreign investment and external assistance. These aspects will be discussed briefly in turn.

In 1950 almost all of the important economic decisions in sub-Saharan Africa, government and private, were in the hands of foreigners. Today, with the significant exception of the transnational corporations, most are in the hands of local people. The extent of foreign control was not as great twenty-five years ago in Asia or Latin America, but there, too, nationalization and increased taxation of foreign enterprises—especially in mining and petroleum activities—has substantially increased local ownership, control, and rents.[2]

Twenty-five years ago most of the African colonies and some countries in Asia and Latin America depended on a small handful of commodities for the bulk of their exports. Today, in many if not most countries, the growth of industrial exports and the diversification of agricultural exports have reduced significantly the degree of commodity concentration of foreign exchange earnings.

The concentration of foreign trade on a single country has also been reduced significantly in most developing countries since 1950.[3] The growth of the European Common Market, Japan, and eastern Europe has played a role in this. So, too, has the increase in trade among developing countries themselves, though such inter-

---

this footnote, see the various readings in Uphoff and Ilchman [1972], Wilber [1973], and Bernstein [1974], as well as the references listed in Meier [1976, pp. 123–24].

2. For empirical evidence on this and some of the following propositions, see Warren [1977].

3. See Kleiman [1976]. Unfortunately, even diversification of trading ties cannot always insulate nations from foreign shocks. Not only India and Tanzania but even Japan and the rich nations of Europe found the limits to their national self-reliance drawn in sharp relief by the oil price rises of 1973–74.

change has expanded less than it might have if the participants had followed more liberal trade policies relating to traditional goods. Formal integration schemes, for which high hopes were held, have been particularly disappointing in this regard. The Latin American Free Trade Area barely got off the ground, the Central American and East African Common Markets have suffered serious politicoeconomic disruptions, and the Andean Group has been experiencing difficulties. In all four cases, disputes over the inequitable distribution of integration-created benefits have been central to their problems.[4] The picture has not all been black, however; in South and Southeast Asia trade among developing countries has been important and growing.

Foreign firms have been more important as a source of capital in some countries than in others. But on balance, foreign direct investment has provided no more than 3 or 4 percent of the total capital requirement of the developing market economies since 1969. Indeed, since 1955 the total contribution of all external capital—foreign private investment, official grant aid, and public and private debt—has generally averaged no more than about 10 percent of the total investment expenditure of the developing market economies.[5] Thus, although the foreign contribution may have been significant at the margin, the great bulk of the development that has taken place since 1950 has been financed by the developing countries themselves.

Aside from their (relatively small) quantitative contribution to the capital needs of the developing countries, foreign investors have also brought with them embodied technology. In some cases this has been welcomed as a modernizing influence that might help the country's producers to compete in world markets, thereby perhaps increasing national economic independence. But

4. For a theoretical analysis of this problem of the distribution of benefits, with particular reference to the Andean Group, see Morawetz [1974a]. For a more optimistic view of the Andean Group's prospects, see Ffrench-Davis [1977].

5. World Bank, unpublished data. The percentage for all developing countries is even lower once China is included.

in other cases it has been criticized as causing technological dependence and as being inappropriate to national factor availabilities. Some countries such as Hong Kong, Singapore, and Taiwan have succeeded in avoiding such technological dependence and in fostering local technology adaptation by adopting an outward-looking trade strategy and keeping prices in line with social costs. By contrast, China has achieved identical ends by following what are, in some respects, diametrically opposite policies: closing off the economy from foreign influence, decentralizing, and fostering a sociocultural climate that is conducive to managers' making socially appropriate decisions.[6] At least during the 1950s and early 1960s many Latin American countries followed a policy somewhere between these two—inward-looking policies with acceptance of foreign investment—and apparently got the worst of both worlds. In developing the ability to adapt technology to local needs, thereby reducing technological dependence, is it perhaps necessary to go to one extreme or the other to succeed?[7]

External debt is sometimes regarded as a particular problem of economic self-reliance and independence. As may be seen in Table 18, the ratio of external public debt to GNP has risen steadily and significantly since the 1950s for a wide range of countries and has jumped sharply since 1973 for a number of oil-importing countries. The ratio of external total debt to GNP must have been rising faster still, because private borrowing has been increasing its share of total debt, at least since 1967.[8] There is considerable diversity within the generally increasing trend, with no noticeable relationship between public debt and size of country or income level. For example, Brazil and India have modest ratios

6. Keesing [1975].

7. Hirschman [1971] and Streeten [1972] have provocative discussions of this subject. See also the other papers surveyed in Morawetz [1974, section III.2].

8. Debt to private lenders—suppliers' credits, borrowing from private banks, and so forth—rose from less than 30 percent of total foreign debt in 1967 to 50 percent in 1976 [World Bank 1977a].

Table 18. External Public Debt Outstanding (Including Undisbursed) as a Percentage of GNP, Selected Countries, Various Years, 1950–75

Country	1950 (1)	1955 (2)	1960 (3)	1965 (4)	1970 (5)	1975 (6)
Africa						
Algeria	n.a.	1.1	1.6	11.8	20.8	34.8
Ghana	n.a.	n.a.	1.4	14.9	22.6	10.1
Ivory Coast	n.a.	n.a.	n.a.	n.a.	18.2	26.9
Kenya	n.a.	10.2	12.5	20.0	18.5	16.8
Morocco	n.a.	10.1	8.7	8.9	21.4	16.8
Senegal	n.a.	n.a.	n.a.	n.a.	12.3	14.5
Sudan	n.a.	n.a.	6.0	11.8	15.8	22.7
Tanzania	n.a.	3.1	3.5	11.7	17.0	30.2
Tunisia	n.a.	n.a.	n.a.	19.2	37.3	24.9
Zambia	n.a.	n.a.	n.a.	n.a.	32.0	43.8
South Asia						
Bangladesh	n.a.	n.a.	n.a.	n.a.	n.a.	12.3
India	0.2	1.3	4.7	10.3	14.8	14.4
Pakistan	n.a.	n.a.	9.6 [a]	37.9 [a]	29.1	44.2
Sri Lanka	3.8	5.2	8.3	13.9	24.5	31.8
East Asia						
Indonesia	n.a.	5.9	n.a.	16.5	32.1	29.8
Korea, Republic of	n.a.	n.a.	n.a.	5.7	22.0	27.9
Malaysia	n.a.	n.a.	5.7	7.3	9.7	14.7
Philippines	n.a.	1.9	2.4	5.5	8.3	8.3
Thailand	1.3	2.1	3.3	5.3	4.9	4.3
Latin America						
Argentina	1.1	2.4	7.1	7.5	7.6	7.4
Bolivia	n.a.	12.6	24.5	23.1	54.8	39.4
Brazil	3.0	5.4	4.7	4.0	8.1	11.5
Colombia	4.5	6.3	7.0	14.7	18.1	18.2
Costa Rica	n.a.	6.9	7.5	16.1	13.8	20.7
Ecuador	3.6	6.1	6.6	10.9	13.2	9.8
Guatemala	n.a.	n.a.	n.a.	n.a.	5.9	4.5
Honduras	n.a.	n.a.	n.a.	n.a.	13.0	23.2
Jamaica	n.a.	n.a.	n.a.	6.7	10.3	22.3
Mexico	3.5	2.5	4.4	5.9	9.8	16.6
Nicaragua	n.a.	n.a.	n.a.	n.a.	19.4	37.4
Paraguay	n.a.	n.a.	n.a.	n.a.	16.7	12.0
Peru	3.2	5.4	5.0	9.6	14.8	21.4

n.a. Not available.
a. Includes Bangladesh.
Sources: Columns 1–3: computed from unpublished data, External Debt Division, World Bank. Columns 4–6: World Bank, *Annual Reports,* 1972 to 1976.

Table 19. Service Payments on Public Debt (Interest and Repayments of Principal) as a Percentage of Exports, Selected Countries, Various Years, 1950–75

Country	1950 (1)	1955 (2)	1960 (3)	1965 (4)	1970 (5)	1975 (6)
Africa						
Algeria	n.a.	n.a.	n.a.	n.a.	3.9	9.8
Ghana	n.a.	n.a.	n.a.	19.0	5.0	4.6
Ivory Coast	n.a.	n.a.	n.a.	4.5	6.1	11.7
Kenya	n.a.	5.0	6.1	5.9	3.7	3.2
Morocco	n.a.	n.a.	n.a.	4.8	8.4	8.3
Senegal	n.a.	n.a.	n.a.	n.a.	2.4	n.a.
Sudan	n.a.	n.a.	2.0	5.5	9.0	18.3
Tanzania	n.a.	n.a.	1.9	4.5	4.9	4.7
Tunisia	n.a.	n.a.	n.a.	7.7	18.6	n.a.
Zambia	n.a.	n.a.	n.a.	2.7	5.4	8.0
South Asia						
Bangladesh	n.a.	n.a.	n.a.	n.a.	n.a.	16.2
India	n.a.	0.9	6.6	15.0	22.0	n.a.
Pakistan	n.a.	8.5 [a]	8.3 [a]	11.0 [a]	22.1 [a]	18.2
Sri Lanka	n.a.	0.5	0.8	2.0	9.6	20.0
East Asia						
Indonesia	n.a.	3.6	n.a.	10.3	6.5	6.7
Korea, Republic of	n.a.	n.a.	n.a.	2.8	21.2	11.2
Malaysia	n.a.	n.a.	2.3	1.3	2.9	3.1
Philippines	n.a.	3.1	2.1	5.4	7.3	7.2
Thailand	n.a.	1.2	4.0	4.4	3.3	2.5
Latin America						
Argentina	1.3	2.9	n.a.	20.2	21.5	22.9
Bolivia	n.a.	5.3	11.6	4.8	10.9	16.6
Brazil	n.a.	20.8	n.a.	12.4	14.1	14.6
Colombia	2.7	7.5	13.6	14.4	11.6	11.7
Costa Rica	n.a.	1.9	6.4	10.3	9.9	10.4
Ecuador	n.a.	4.3	7.9	7.5	9.0	4.6
Guatemala	n.a.	n.a.	n.a.	5.2	7.6	2.0
Honduras	n.a.	n.a.	n.a.	2.4	2.8	4.5
Jamaica	n.a.	n.a.	n.a.	1.9	3.1	6.8
Mexico	7.2	10.8	20.1	24.8	23.6	26.0
Nicaragua	n.a.	n.a.	n.a.	4.3	10.4	11.7
Paraguay	n.a.	n.a.	n.a.	4.2	11.1	9.7
Peru	3.2	6.5	12.0	6.8	13.6	22.5

n.a. Not available.
a. Includes Bangladesh.
Sources: Same as Table 18.

of public debt to GNP, 12 and 14 percent, respectively, whereas Pakistan has a ratio of 44 percent.[9]

Despite this across-the-board increase in the ratio of debt to GNP, the rapid rise in exports from developing countries has helped to check the proportion of exports needed to service public debt (Table 19). In Brazil, Colombia, Ecuador, and Kenya this proportion actually seems to have fallen between 1960 (or 1955) and 1975, while only in Argentina, Mexico, Peru, and Sri Lanka did it reach 20 percent by the latter date.[10]

In summary, although in recent years much attention has been paid to the problems of technological dependence and debt, these (in some cases) real problems should not in the longer term evaluation be allowed to obscure the basic and important progress that has been made toward economic self-reliance in a wide spectrum of developing countries. This has been particularly noticeable in increased national control of the economy, diversification of foreign ties, and reduced dependence on a small number of export products as sources of foreign exchange.

9. Indebtedness of developing countries is quite highly concentrated. Brazil, India, and Mexico alone accounted for about 35 percent of total debt in 1974. In the same year, of eighty-one countries for which data are available, eighteen accounted for 80 percent of total debt [World Bank 1977a].

10. It is not clear at what point the ratio of debt service to exports becomes undesirably high; more work might usefully be done on this question. For some of the earlier literature on foreign borrowing, most of which does not incorporate explicitly the self-reliance objective, see Avramovic [1958], Avramovic and Gulhati [1960], Hamada [1965], and Bardhan [1967 and 1970]. See also Pearson Report [1969] and Klein [1972].

5

Conclusions, Hypotheses, and Questions

History therefore consists not of facts but of historians' opinions of what happened, and of why it happened.

LEWIS [*1955, p. 15*]

IN AVERAGE PER CAPITA INCOME the developing countries grew more rapidly between 1950 and 1975—3.4 percent a year—than either they or the developed countries had done in any comparable period in the past. They thereby exceeded both official goals and private expectations. That this growth was real and not simply statistical artifact may be seen in the progress that occurred simultaneously in various indexes of basic needs. Increases in life expectancy that required a century of economic development in the industrialized countries have been achieved in the developing world in two or three decades. Progress has been made in the eradication of communicable diseases. And the proportion of adults in developing countries who are literate has increased substantially.[1]

---

1. A referee adds a reminder that, at a more impressionistic level, "evidence of progress in many of the developing countries is available to the naked eye in the form of better-fed and better-dressed school children;

This impressive average growth and development performance masks a wide diversity of experience. In one group of nations average per capita income roughly trebled between 1950 and 1975, with the increase being spread widely throughout society in most cases. This group has a combined population of close to 1 billion—35 percent of the developing world—and includes China, Hong Kong, Korea, Singapore, Taiwan and a number of the OPEC countries.

In a second set of countries—including Pakistan, the Philippines, Thailand, Turkey, some OPEC countries and much of Latin America, and incorporating about 25 percent of the developing world's population—growth was moderate to rapid. But in these nations there was an unequal and in some cases increasingly unequal distribution of the benefits of growth.

Finally, a third set of countries experienced slow growth and a relatively unequal distribution of such increments to income as were available. This group includes much of South Asia and some of the poorer parts of Africa and incorporates about 40 percent of the developing world's people. Many of the poorest persons in these countries, and some of those in the second group as well, improved their economic situation very little during the twenty-five years; although the issue is in dispute, signficant numbers of them may even have become worse off in absolute terms.

What can be learned from the experience of the past twenty-five years, and what are some of the hypotheses and questions suggested by it?

Many Roads Lead to Development, but . . .

Clearly, there is more than one feasible route to equitable growth and development. Some countries have succeeded by pursuing

---

more radios and bicycles and clinics; buses patronized by persons who previously trudged along on foot; trucks laden with things [that people] previously carried on their backs and heads; etc. etc. Such supporting evidence need not be ruled out as inherently less trustworthy or interesting than numbers accumulated, God knows how, by national statistical offices determined to satisfy the insatiable appetites of the United Nations and the World Bank."

market-oriented, outward-looking strategies, relying on entrepreneurial skills (Taiwan, Korea, and Hong Kong) or physical resources (oil exporters) as the keys to growth. By contrast, China has followed a socialist, inward-looking strategy based on considerable natural resources, ideology, and highly effective social organization.

Does this mean that each country can select its own socioeconomic system from the full menu of choices? Or do large, poor countries that wish to eradicate poverty necessarily have to follow a route such as China's? What about small trade-dependent economies: do they have any realistic option other than to follow the Taiwan-Korea route? A number of smaller countries— Burma, Cuba, North Korea, Sri Lanka, and Tanzania, to name a few—have tried to follow basic needs oriented paths: to what extent are they succeeding? In general, is it possible to follow a strategy oriented to equality and basic needs without closing off the economy as China and some of the smaller socialist countries did? If the economy is not closed off, how can talented people be prevented from leaving (other than by distorting the domestic income distribution) and how can the generation and local adaptation of technology be fostered?

Decentralization and Entrepreneurship

Despite their obvious differences, the Taiwan-Korea group of countries and China share significant similarities. In particular, although the various national governments played an important role in establishing an overall policy framework to send appropriate signals to lower-level decisionmakers, the bulk of the day-to-day economic decisions were made at a decentralized local level without a great deal of interference from the central government. This division of functions by level seems to have been logical and effective. By contrast, in a number of countries in which the central government got itself involved in detailed decisionmaking at a lower level—whether by production- and import-licensing in a market-oriented system or by detailed planning and programming in a socialist one—the result was often a combination of red tape, bureaucratic delay, and arbitrary decisions that stifled initiative.

Whatever the underlying political philosophy, a decentralized system of decisionmaking relies heavily for success upon the response of the local functionaries to centrally determined incentives. In a market-oriented system these functionaries are the entrepreneurs and managers; in a socialist one they are the local officials. Many developing countries seem to have an abundant supply of petty entrepreneurs—small traders and informal sector producers—but only in a few cases are there significant numbers of larger-scale operators. What are the factors that determine the growth of medium- to large-scale entrepreneurship? And what kind of policy intervention can help to foster it? [2] Although something is already known on the subject, more work might also profitably be done on the ways in which socialist systems have succeeded (and failed) in the parallel task of motivating local officials to take initiatives and make socially appropriate decisions.

Growth and Poverty

Although it is true that some of the poorest people in some developing countries may have become worse off in absolute terms since 1950, the blame can hardly be laid on economic growth; countries in which many people have (or may have) become worse off include at least as many slow growers as fast growers. Indeed, for poor, heavily populated nations such as India, Bangladesh, Pakistan, and Indonesia, only long-term, sustained, equitably distributed growth of per capita income offers the majority of the people any hope of economic advancement.

2. There is a large early literature on entrepreneurship: see, for example, Schumpeter [1936], Leibenstein [1957], Gerschenkron [1962], and Papanek [1962]; also Baumol [1968], Epstein [1970], Harris [1970], Hill [1970], Watanabe [1970], Kilby [1971], Nafziger [1975 and 1977], and Hughes [1976]—and in general, on noneconomic factors in development—Hoselitz [1956], McClelland [1961], and Hagen [1962]. But unfortunately these subjects largely went out of fashion at about the same time as quantification came in. Perhaps definition of the success of the Taiwan-Korea group of countries partly in terms of entrepreneurship may regain for this specialization the place that it deserves.

Redistribution before Growth?

Many of the countries that experienced rapid, equitably distributed growth between 1950 and 1975 began the period with relatively equal distributions of assets and incomes; many of those which experienced rapid, inequitably distributed growth started out with sharply unequal distributions. This suggests that the initial distribution of assets and incomes may be an important determinant of the trend in inequality. Such a hypothesis makes some intuitive sense. People who own assets, whether physical or human capital, are in the best place to profit once growth begins. Furthermore, both historical and simulation evidence suggest that the most powerful determinant of the income distribution is the underlying structure of the economy; once growth is taking place, it seems to be difficult to redistribute income effectively through the use of such marginalist instruments as taxation and public employment.

These combined observations have potentially powerful implications. In particular, if a relatively high degree of equality is to be a short- to medium-term goal, it simply may not be possible to "grow first and redistribute later." Rather, it may be necessary to tackle asset redistribution as a first priority by whatever means are at hand. There exists a vast and easily accessible literature on the subject of how to grow: on what policies have been tried, where, and with what results.[3] But on the question of how to redistribute, the contributions, though many, are more disparate. It may be useful at this stage for some persons knowledgeable in the field to draw the threads together. In general, which land reforms and other redistributions of assets have worked, which have not, and why? Based on historical experience, is it possible to

3. For example, for recent work on the Taiwan-Korea model, see Fei, Ranis, and Kuo [1976] and Westphal [1977]; on resource-based development, see Roemer [1977]; and on trade policies and development, see Little, Scitovsky, and Scott [1970], Balassa [1971], Díaz-Alejandro [1973], Balassa [1977], and the volumes by Bhagwati [1978] and Krueger [1978] summarizing the series of country studies from the National Bureau for Economic Research.

draw up a list of necessary (and sufficient?) conditions for each type of asset redistribution to be successful? What has been the relationship, if any, between different types of redistribution and subsequent experience with growth?

Political Stability

The historical experience suggests that political stability, of whatever ilk, and stability of the economic "rules of the game" may be an important and underrated determinant of economic growth. Most of the countries that grew fastest during the period had such stability; many of the slowest growers conspicuously did not. Bolivia provides an interesting example in this regard. To oversimplify the case: up to 1970, Bolivia had had 184 governments in 146 years, and its growth rate during 1950–70 was one of the slowest in the developing world. Then a period of unusual political stability began, and after a short period the growth rate accelerated significantly. Political stability would, of course, be a necessary but not sufficient condition for growth—as any one of a number of stable, stagnant countries might testify.

Costs

Nowhere in this study has there been mention of the differential personal and social costs associated with different strategies of development. To some extent this omission is excusable: for people living at subsistence level, bread is surely more important than civil rights. But after subsistence has been assured, is more bread always preferable (and preferred) to more freedom? True, the benefits from civil rights and personal freedoms and the costs associated with their absence cannot easily be quantified. But that does not mean that they are of no importance in an overall evaluation of the development that has taken place.

Expectations

The historical experience illustrates a tendency for rapid interaction to occur between development performance and expectations. "Upper-limit" projections have been surpassed, "almost unmeetable challenges" have been met; yet everywhere there is dissatisfaction. It might be useful to bear in mind that first-round successes (improvements in health, the Green Revolution) often lead to second-round problems (population explosion, worsening of rural income distribution), and that even in the best of cases, development is a long, slow process measured in generations rather than decades.

There is one more lesson to be learned from the historical experience with development, the most powerful—though not the most helpful for policy purposes—lesson of all. Take one more look at the state in 1950 of what are now called the developing countries. Among the most populous of them, China was recovering from decades of foreign domination and then violent revolution; India and Pakistan had recently received independence, in the process going through a bloody partition with massive cross-migrations and communal killings. Bangladesh was not yet born, Nigeria was under foreign rule, and Indonesia had been free of foreign control for two years. Brazil and Mexico had had rather more political stability and continuity, but Brazil still had largely a one-crop economy that relied on coffee for 60 percent of its export earnings, compared with 10 percent in 1975.

Among those nations which are today regarded as some of the success stories of development, Taiwan and one-year-old Israel were recovering from occupation or war and from huge influxes of population that were to make a lasting mark on the national characters of the two nations. The Korean peninsula was newly divided and at war; Singapore was not yet independent; and the country whose per capita income was to grow faster than any other in the next twenty-five years was regarded as undevelopable. "If Libya can be brought to a stage of sustained growth," wrote Higgins in 1959 after working there, "there is hope for every country in the world" [p. 36].

All of which serves as a reminder of what somebody once called the one great lesson of history:

Things were not always the way they are now,
nor will they forever remain so.

Statistical Appendix

Table A1. Annual Growth Rate of GNP per Capita, by Region and Country, 1950–75

Region and country	GNP per capita (1974 U.S. dollars) 1950 [b] (1)	1975 (2)	Annual growth rate [a] (percent) 1950–60 (3)	1960–70 (4)	1970–75 (5)	1950–75 (6)
Africa	170	308	2.4	2.2	2.8	2.4
Algeria [c]	484	718	4.4	−0.7	3.6	1.6
Angola	226	623	5.8	3.7	3.1	4.2
Benin, People's Republic of	n.a.	125	n.a.	0.8	−0.5	n.a.
Botswana	141	300	0.8	3.3	3.8	3.1
Burundi	117	91	−3.3	1.1	0.3	−1.0
Cameroon	133	246	1.5	4.4	−0.3	2.5
Central African Empire	202	212	0.5	0.3	−0.7	0.2
Chad	n.a.	111	n.a.	−0.9	−2.0	n.a.
Congo, People's Republic of	303	460	−0.8	2.2	4.7	1.7
Egypt, Arab Republic of	203	286	0.9	1.6	1.4	1.4
Ethiopia	58	94	2.3	2.7	0.5	2.0
Gabon [c]	n.a.	2,061	n.a.	3.3	7.8	n.a.
Gambia, The	99	178	−0.2	3.8	5.9	2.4
Ghana	354	427	1.9	−0.7	−0.1	0.7
Guinea	n.a.	118	n.a.	0.0	1.0	n.a.
Ivory Coast	283	460	−0.0	4.3	1.3	2.0
Kenya	129	200	1.0	3.2	2.5	1.8
Lesotho	n.a.	161	n.a.	4.7	7.4	n.a.
Liberia	n.a.	377	n.a.	1.1	0.0	n.a.
Libyan Arab Republic [c]	786	4,675	1.1	17.3	5.3	7.4
Madagascar	195	180	−0.1	0.2	−2.2	−0.3
Malawi	68	137	1.6	2.7	6.4	2.8
Mali	67	87	1.2	1.2	−0.0	1.1
Mauritania	200	288	−2.6	5.6	2.6	1.5
Mauritius	575	533	−3.1	−0.6	4.9	−0.3
Morocco	353	435	−0.7	1.3	2.9	0.8
Mozambique	177	284	3.9	2.9	−3.3	1.9
Niger	n.a.	122	n.a.	−0.5	−3.5	n.a.
Nigeria [c]	150	287	2.1	0.4	3.8	2.6
Rhodesia	n.a.	499	n.a.	0.7	2.6	n.a.
Rwanda	119	81	−1.8	−0.8	−4.4	−1.6
Senegal	238	341	4.4	−1.6	1.1	1.5
Sierra Leone	n.a.	181	2.5	n.a.	0.0	n.a.
Somalia	37	92	10.6	−1.1	−0.2	3.7
Sudan	118	267	2.7	−0.7	15.4	3.3
Swaziland	79	434	5.9	6.4	8.0	7.0
Tanzania	84	160	3.7	3.0	0.6	2.6
Togo	164	245	−1.4	5.7	1.4	1.6

Table A1 (*continued*)

Region and country	GNP per capita (1974 U.S. dollars) 1950 [b] (1)	1975 (2)	Annual growth rate [a] (percent) 1950–60 (3)	1960–70 (4)	1970–75 (5)	1950–75 (6)
Tunisia	n.a.	695	1.2	2.1	7.2	n.a.
Uganda	195	229	0.8	3.0	−3.1	0.6
Upper Volta	99	87	−0.7	0.6	−2.8	−0.5
Zaïre	94	139	1.1	2.4	1.1	1.6
Zambia	310	495	2.7	3.2	−0.5	1.9
South Asia	*(85)*	*132*	*2.7*	*1.5*	*−0.4*	*1.7*
Afghanistan	89	119	1.8	0.0	2.5	1.2
Bangladesh	n.a.	103	n.a.	1.0	−2.3	n.a.
Burma	57	100	4.5	0.5	0.8	2.3
India	95	139	2.3	1.4	−0.4	1.5
Nepal	88	102	0.9	0.7	0.1	0.7
Pakistan	n.a.	131	n.a.	4.2	0.3	n.a.
Sri Lanka	90	134	1.3	2.4	1.1	1.6
East Asia	*130*	*341*	*3.3*	*4.0*	*4.8*	*3.9*
British Solomon Islands	n.a.	307	n.a.	1.4	1.9	n.a.
China (Taiwan)	224	817	4.8	5.9	5.8	5.3
Fiji	571	842	−0.4	1.7	4.8	1.6
Hong Kong	470	1,584	3.6	7.6	4.2	5.0
Indonesia [c]	103	169	1.6	1.4	3.6	2.0
Khmer Republic	112	(80)	1.7	0.8	−12.1	(−1.4)
Korea, Republic of	146	504	2.6	6.4	8.3	5.1
Lao People's Democratic Republic	62	(68)	−0.5	1.9	−0.5	(0.3)
Malaysia	350	665	0.8	3.9	4.3	2.6
Papua New Guinea	229	412	1.7	4.0	2.2	2.3
Philippines	168	340	3.2	2.1	3.5	2.8
Singapore	n.a.	2,307	n.a.	6.2	7.3	n.a.
Thailand	132	319	2.6	5.0	3.6	3.6
Vietnam	143	163	1.7	n.a.	n.a.	0.5
Middle East	*(460)*	*1,660*	*4.0*	*5.7*	*7.9*	*(5.2)*
Bahrain	n.a.	2,244	n.a.	n.a.	22.0	n.a.
Iran [c]	384	1,321	3.0	5.9	8.9	5.1
Iraq [c]	283	1,180	6.7	3.0	12.1	5.9
Israel	1,090	3,287	4.5	5.0	3.3	4.5
Jordan	186	423	6.1	3.3	−1.0	3.3
Kuwait [c]	19,160	10,590	−1.8	−1.5	−4.4	−2.3
Lebanon	690	n.a.	0.2	2.4	5.1	n.a.
Oman	n.a.	1,903	n.a.	11.4	19.4	n.a.
Qatar [c]	n.a.	7,655	n.a.	3.1	12.0	n.a.
Saudi Arabia [c]	n.a.	2,767	n.a.	7.5	13.6	n.a.

Table A1 (*continued*)

Region and country	GNP per capita (1974 U.S. dollars) 1950 [b] (1)	1975 (2)	Annual growth rate [a] (percent) 1950–60 (3)	1960–70 (4)	1970–75 (5)	1950–75 (6)
Syrian Arab Republic	283	604	−0.2	3.8	6.5	3.1
United Arab Emirates [c]	n.a.	9,635	n.a.	19.4	3.7	n.a.
Yemen Arab Republic	n.a.	n.a.	n.a.	n.a.	n.a.	n.a.
Yemen People's Democratic Republic	n.a.	224	n.a.	−1.6	−2.4	n.a.
Latin America	*495*	*944*	*2.1*	*2.5*	*3.7*	*2.6*
Argentina	907	1,464	1.4	2.5	2.1	1.9
Barbados	402	1,155	4.8	5.7	0.5	4.3
Belize	424	700	2.2	2.1	1.5	2.0
Bolivia	244	290	−2.1	2.6	3.2	0.7
Brazil	373	927	3.1	2.3	6.8	3.7
Chile	596	700	1.2	1.8	−2.6	0.7
Colombia	308	510	1.3	2.0	3.6	2.0
Costa Rica	445	834	2.6	2.2	3.5	2.6
Dominican Republic	324	661	2.2	1.4	6.6	2.9
Ecuador [c]	276	503	1.9	2.2	6.4	2.5
El Salvador	263	418	1.6	2.3	2.1	1.9
Guatemala	345	602	0.7	2.9	4.3	2.3
Guyana	383	512	1.3	1.5	0.4	1.2
Haiti	n.a.	163	n.a.	−0.8	1.5	n.a.
Honduras	272	322	0.4	1.9	0.2	0.7
Jamaica	376	1,185	6.8	2.7	4.1	4.7
Mexico	562	1,092	2.4	3.7	2.2	2.7
Netherlands Antilles	1,914	1,595	−1.1	−0.9	0.5	−0.7
Nicaragua	313	661	2.5	4.0	3.0	3.0
Panama	484	977	1.9	4.5	1.0	2.9
Paraguay	354	525	0.4	1.6	3.8	1.6
Peru	403	748	2.6	1.9	2.7	2.5
Surinam	n.a.	1,187	n.a.	4.6	2.2	n.a.
Trinidad and Tobago	713	1,746	6.0	2.0	2.6	3.7
Uruguay	978	1,220	−1.5	0.4	−0.1	0.9
Venezuela [c]	992	2,045	3.5	2.5	2.4	2.9
Southern Europe	*(520)*	*1,580*	*4.6*	*4.5*	*4.4*	*(4.5)*
Cyprus	638	1,082	2.1	5.6	−3.9	2.1
Greece	556	2,173	4.8	6.9	4.1	5.4
Malta	412	1,250	2.7	5.5	8.3	4.6
Portugal	n.a.	1,479	n.a.	n.a.	n.a.	n.a.
Romania	n.a.	1,543	n.a.	4.4	5.4	n.a.
Spain	710	2,487	5.3	5.0	5.1	5.1
Turkey	316	793	3.5	3.5	5.0	3.7
Yugoslavia	429	1,364	4.4	4.4	5.4	4.7

Table A1 (*continued*)

Region and country	GNP per capita (1974 U.S. dollars) 1950 [b] (1)	1975 (2)	Annual growth rate [a] (percent) 1950– 60 (3)	1960– 70 (4)	1970– 75 (5)	1950– 75 (6)
OPEC countries [c]	(200)	648	(4.2)	4.6	6.9	(4.8)
OECD countries [d]	2,378	5,238	3.0	4.1	2.3	3.2
Australia	2,998	5,190	1.5	3.2	2.4	2.2
Austria	1,409	4,343	5.5	3.9	4.0	4.6
Belgium	2,406	5,578	2.4	4.1	3.9	3.4
Canada	3,374	6,112	1.2	3.7	3.2	2.4
Denmark	3,104	6,366	2.5	4.0	1.8	2.9
Finland	1,690	4,686	3.9	4.1	4.1	4.2
France	2,064	5,294	3.5	4.3	3.2	3.8
Germany, Federal Republic of	2,005	6,080	6.8	3.7	1.7	4.5
Iceland	2,762	5,172	2.6	2.8	2.5	2.6
Ireland	1,175	2,225	2.2	3.8	1.2	2.6
Italy	935	2,704	5.4	4.7	1.8	4.3
Japan	659	4,105	7.3	9.4	4.3	7.6
Luxembourg	3,542	5,568	1.7	2.6	1.2	1.8
Netherlands, The	2,312	5,143	3.2	3.9	2.4	3.3
New Zealand	3,054	4,303	0.8	2.2	1.0	1.4
Norway	2,697	6,018	2.6	3.8	3.3	3.3
Sweden	3,442	7,243	2.8	3.7	2.2	3.0
Switzerland	3,938	7,401	3.0	2.9	0.8	2.6
United Kingdom	2,064	3,532	2.4	2.3	2.1	2.2
United States	3,954	6,495	1.5	3.3	1.7	2.0
South Africa	696	1,211	1.7	3.2	1.8	2.2

n.a. Not available.

a. Growth rates for 1960–70 and 1970–75 for individual countries are least square estimates. In all other cases, because of lack of data, they are end-point estimates.

b. GNP per capita for 1950 is estimated by applying the growth rate of GDP per capita in 1950–60 (World Bank, *World Tables 1976*) to figures for GNP per capita in 1960 (*World Bank Atlas, 1977*).

c. OPEC members: Algeria, Ecuador, Gabon, Indonesia, Iran, Iraq, Kuwait, Libyan Arab Republic, Nigeria, Qatar, Saudi Arabia, United Arab Emirates, Venezuela.

d. All OECD members except Greece, Portugal, Spain, and Turkey.

Sources: Column 1: see note b., above. Column 2: Data tapes, *World Bank Atlas* (1977). Column 3: World Bank, *World Tables 1976*. Columns 4,5: Computed from *Atlas*. Column 6: Computed from estimated 1950 figures and 1975 figures from *Atlas* (1975).

Table A2. Annual Growth Rate of GNP per Capita, by Income Group and Country, 1950–75

Income group and country	Annual growth rate [a] (percent)			
	1950–60	*1960–70*	*1970–75*	*1950–75* [b]
Lower-income countries ($265 GNP per capita or less)	*(1.4)*	*1.6*	*−0.2*	*(1.1)*
Afghanistan	1.8	0.0	2.5	1.2
Bangladesh	n.a.	1.0	−2.3	n.a.
Benin, People's Republic of	n.a.	0.8	−0.5	n.a.
Burma	4.5	0.5	0.8	2.3
Burundi	−3.3	1.1	0.3	−1.0
Central African Empire	0.5	0.3	−0.7	0.2
Chad	n.a.	−0.9	−2.0	n.a.
Ethiopia	2.3	2.7	0.5	2.0
Gambia, The	−0.2	3.8	5.9	2.4
Guinea	n.a.	0.0	1.0	n.a.
Haiti	n.a.	−0.8	1.5	n.a.
India	2.3	1.4	−0.4	1.5
Indonesia	1.6	1.4	3.6	2.0
Kenya	1.0	3.2	2.5	1.8
Khmer Republic	1.7	0.8	−12.1	(−1.4)
Lao People's Democratic Republic	−0.5	1.9	−0.5	(0.3)
Lesotho	n.a.	4.7	7.4	n.a.
Madagascar	−0.1	0.2	−2.2	−0.3
Malawi	1.6	2.7	6.4	2.8
Mali	1.2	1.2	−0.0	1.1
Nepal	0.9	0.7	0.1	0.7
Niger	n.a.	−0.5	−3.5	n.a.
Pakistan	n.a.	4.2	0.3	n.a.
Rwanda	−1.8	−0.8	−4.4	−1.6
Sierra Leone	2.5	n.a.	0.0	n.a.
Somalia	10.6	−1.1	−0.2	3.7
Sri Lanka	1.3	2.4	1.1	1.6
Tanzania	3.7	3.0	0.6	2.6
Uganda	0.8	3.1	−3.1	0.6
Vietnam	1.7	n.a.	n.a.	0.5
Yemen Arab Republic	n.a.	n.a.	n.a.	n.a.
Yemen People's Democratic Republic	n.a.	−1.6	−2.4	n.a.
Zaïre	1.1	2.4	1.1	1.6

Table A2 (*continued*)

Income group and country	Annual growth rate [a] (percent)			
	1950–60	*1960–70*	*1970–75*	*1950–75* [b]
Middle-income countries				
($266–$520 GNP per capita)	2.2	2.0	2.9	2.4
Bolivia	−2.1	2.6	3.2	0.7
Botswana	0.8	3.3	3.8	3.1
British Solomon Islands	n.a.	1.4	1.9	n.a.
Cameroon	1.5	4.4	−0.3	2.5
Congo, People's Republic of	−0.8	2.2	4.7	1.7
Egypt, Arab Republic of	0.9	1.6	1.4	1.4
El Salvador	1.6	2.3	2.1	1.9
Ghana	1.9	−0.7	−0.1	0.7
Honduras	0.4	1.9	0.2	0.7
Ivory Coast	−0.0	4.3	1.3	2.0
Jordan	6.1	3.3	−1.0	3.3
Liberia	n.a.	1.1	0.0	n.a.
Mauritania	−2.6	5.6	2.6	1.5
Morocco	−0.7	1.3	2.9	0.8
Mozambique	3.9	2.9	−3.3	1.9
Nigeria	2.1	0.4	3.8	2.6
Papua New Guinea	1.7	4.0	2.2	2.3
Philippines	3.2	2.1	3.5	2.8
Rhodesia	n.a.	0.7	2.6	n.a.
Senegal	4.4	−1.6	1.1	1.5
Sudan	2.7	−0.7	15.4	3.3
Swaziland	5.9	6.4	8.0	7.0
Thailand	2.6	5.0	3.6	3.6
Togo	−1.4	5.7	1.4	1.6
Upper–middle-income countries				
($521–$1,075 GNP per capita)	2.4	3.2	4.8	3.4
Algeria	4.4	−0.7	3.6	1.6
Angola	5.8	3.7	3.1	4.2
Belize	2.2	2.1	1.5	2.0
Brazil	3.1	2.3	6.8	3.7
Chile	1.2	1.8	−2.6	0.7
China (Taiwan)	4.8	5.9	5.8	5.3
Colombia	1.3	2.0	3.6	2.0
Costa Rica	2.6	2.2	3.5	2.6
Dominican Republic	2.2	1.4	6.6	2.9
Ecuador	1.9	2.2	6.4	2.5
Fiji	−0.4	1.7	4.8	1.6
Guatemala	0.7	2.9	4.3	2.3
Guyana	1.3	1.5	0.4	1.2
Korea, Republic of	2.6	6.4	8.3	5.1
Malaysia	0.8	3.9	4.3	2.6
Mauritius	−3.1	−0.6	4.9	−0.3

Table A2 (*continued*)

Income group and country	Annual growth rate[a] (percent)			
	1950–60	*1960–70*	*1970–75*	*1950–75* [b]
Mexico	2.4	3.7	2.2	2.7
Nicaragua	2.5	4.0	3.0	3.0
Panama	1.9	4.5	1.0	2.9
Paraguay	0.4	1.6	3.8	1.6
Peru	2.6	1.9	2.7	2.5
Syrian Arab Republic	−0.2	3.8	6.5	3.1
Tunisia	1.2	2.1	7.2	n.a.
Turkey	3.5	3.5	5.0	3.7
Zambia	2.7	3.2	−0.5	1.9
Higher-income countries *(over $1,075 GNP per capita)*	*3.2*	*5.8*	*5.7*	*(5.2)*
Argentina	1.4	2.5	2.1	1.9
Bahamas	n.a.	n.a.	n.a.	n.a.
Bahrain	n.a.	n.a.	22.0	n.a.
Barbados	4.8	5.7	0.5	4.3
Cyprus	2.1	5.6	−3.9	2.1
Gabon	n.a.	3.3	7.8	n.a.
Greece	4.8	6.9	4.1	5.4
Hong Kong	3.6	7.6	4.2	5.0
Iran	3.0	5.9	8.9	5.1
Iraq	6.7	3.0	12.1	5.9
Jamaica	6.8	2.7	4.1	4.7
Lebanon	0.2	2.4	5.1	n.a.
Libya	1.1	17.3	5.3	7.4
Kuwait	−1.8	−1.5	−4.4	−2.3
Malta	2.7	5.5	8.3	4.6
Netherlands Antilles	−1.1	−0.9	0.5	−0.7
Oman	n.a.	11.4	19.4	n.a.
Qatar	n.a.	3.1	12.0	n.a.
Saudi Arabia	n.a.	7.5	13.6	n.a.
Singapore	n.a.	6.2	7.3	n.a.
Spain	5.3	5.0	5.1	5.1
Surinam	n.a.	4.6	2.2	n.a.
Trinidad and Tobago	6.0	2.0	2.6	3.7
United Arab Emirates	n.a.	19.4	3.7	n.a.
Uruguay	−1.5	0.4	−0.1	0.9
Venezuela	3.5	2.5	2.4	2.9
Yugoslavia	4.4	4.4	5.4	4.7

n.a. Not available.

a. Growth rates for 1960–70 and 1970–75 for individual countries are least square estimates. In all other cases they are, because of lack of data, end-point estimates.

b. GNP per capita for 1950 is estimated by applying the growth rate of GDP per capita in 1950–60 (World Bank, *World Tables 1976*) to figures for GNP per capita in 1960 (*World Bank Atlas, 1977*).

Sources: Same as columns 3–6 of Table A1.

Table A3. Distribution of Rates of Growth of GNP per Capita, by Region, 1950–75

Region	Annual growth rate, 1950–75	Number of countries growing at			
		Negative to 2 percent	2–4 percent	4–6 percent	6–8 percent
South Asia	1.7	4	1	0	0
Africa	2.4	22	8	1	2
Latin America	2.6	11	11	2	0
East Asia	3.9	5	4	3	0
Middle East	5.2	1	2	3	0
Developing countries	3.4	43	26	9	2

Sources: Table A1.

Table A4. Comparison of the Rosenstein-Rodan Projections (1961) of GNP in 1976 with Actual Figures for 1975

Country	GNP per capita (1974 U.S. dollars) Rosenstein-Rodan projection for 1976 (1)	Actual, 1975 (2)	Ratio (2)÷(1) (3)	Error [a] (4)
Africa				
Algeria	467	718	1.55	—
Angola	166	623	3.75	—
Ethiopia	191	94	0.49	+
Gambia, The	122	178	1.47	—
Ghana	344	427	1.24	—
Kenya	236	200	0.85	+
Liberia	199	377	1.89	—
Libyan Arab Republic	141	4,675	33.16	—
Madagascar	236	180	0.76	+
Mauritius	500	533	1.06	0
Morocco	284	435	1.53	—
Mozambique	191	284	1.48	—
Nigeria	211	287	1.36	—
Rhodesia	433	499	1.15	—
Somalia	133	92	0.69	+
Sudan	189	267	1.41	—
Togo	128	245	1.92	0
Tunisia	348	695	2.00	—
Uganda	176	229	1.31	—
South Asia				
Afghanistan	147	119	0.81	+
Burma	175	100	0.57	+
India	213	139	0.65	+
Nepal	112	102	0.91	0
Pakistan	174	131	0.75	+
Sri Lanka	289	134	0.46	+
East Asia				
China (Taiwan)	258	817	3.16	—
Hong Kong	488	1,584	3.24	—
Indonesia	217	169	0.78	+
Korea, Republic of	250	504	2.01	—
Malaysia	876	665	0.76	+
Philippines	459	340	0.74	+
Singapore	859	2,307	2.69	—
Thailand	235	319	1.36	—
Vietnam	265	163	0.62	+

Table A4 (*continued*)

Country	GNP per capita (1974 U.S. dollars)			
	Rosenstein-Rodan projection for 1976 (1)	Actual, 1975 (2)	Ratio (2)÷(1) (3)	Error [a] (4)
Middle East				
Bahrain	416	2,244	5.39	—
Iran	296	1,321	4.46	—
Iraq	431	1,180	2.73	—
Israel	1,767	3,287	1.86	—
Jordan	253	423	1.67	—
Kuwait	6,554	10,590	1.62	—
Oman	133	1,903	14.26	—
Saudi Arabia	358	2,767	7.73	—
Syrian Arab Republic	394	604	1.53	—
Latin America				
Argentina	1,507	1,464	0.97	0
Bolivia	184	290	1.57	—
Brazil	666	927	1.39	—
Chile	851	700	0.82	+
Colombia	748	510	0.68	+
Costa Rica	557	834	1.50	—
Dominican Republic	493	661	1.35	—
Ecuador	353	503	1.43	—
El Salvador	393	418	1.06	0
Guatemala	382	602	1.57	—
Guyana	453	512	1.13	—
Haiti	222	163	0.74	+
Honduras	373	322	0.86	+
Jamaica	892	1,185	1.33	—
Mexico	746	1,092	1.46	—
Netherlands Antilles	281	1,595	7.64	—
Nicaragua	421	661	1.57	—
Panama	563	977	1.74	—
Paraguay	301	525	1.74	—
Peru	401	748	1.87	—

Table A4 (*continued*)

| Country | GNP per capita (1974 U.S. dollars) | | | |
	Rosenstein-Rodan projection for 1976 (1)	Actual, 1975 (2)	Ratio (2)÷(1) (3)	Error [a] (4)
Surinam	449	1,187	2.64	—
Trinidad and Tobago	894	1,746	1.95	—
Uruguay	1,194	1,220	1.02	0
Venezuela	1,432	2,045	1.43	—

Sources: Column 1: Rosenstein-Rodan (1961), p. 126, column 4, multiplied by 1.93 to bring it to 1974 dollars. Column 2: data tapes, *World Bank Atlas* (1977).

a. $+$ = projection too high; $-$ = projection too low; 0 = projection "correct," that is, up to 10 percent above or below actual 1975 figure. The results may be summarized as follows:

| Region | Number of times projection is | | | |
	Too high (+)	Correct (0)	Too low (−)	Total
Africa	4	2	13	19
South Asia	5	1	0	6
East Asia	4	0	4	8
Middle East	0	0	9	9
Latin America	4	3	17	24
Developing countries	17	6	43	66

Table A5. Comparison of Chenery-Strout Projections of Growth Rates of GNP, 1962–75, with Actual Figures for 1975

Country	Annual GNP growth rates, 1962–75 [a]				
	Actual (1)	Chenery-Strout plan estimate [b] (2)	Error [c] (3)	Chenery-Strout upper limit estimate [d] (4)	Error [c] (5)
Africa					
Algeria	6.9	3.5	−3.4	5.0	−1.9
Egypt, Arab Republic of	3.7	5.5	+1.8	6.0	+2.3
Ethiopia	4.2	4.5	0.3	5.0	+0.8
Ghana	2.4	5.5	+3.1	6.0	+3.6
Kenya	6.7	3.5	−3.2	5.0	−1.7
Liberia	6.1	6.0	0.1	6.0	0.1
Mauritius	2.4	3.4	+1.0	3.4	+1.0
Morocco	4.5	4.0	0.5	6.0	+1.5
Nigeria	6.4	4.5	−1.9	5.0	−1.4
Rhodesia	5.8	4.0	−1.8	4.5	−1.3
Sudan	5.8	5.5	0.3	5.5	0.3
Tanzania	5.2	5.0	0.2	5.6	0.4
Tunisia	6.8	5.0	−1.8	6.0	−0.8
South Asia					
Burma	2.9	4.0	+1.1	5.0	+2.1
India	3.4	5.3	+1.9	6.5	+3.1
Pakistan	6.0	5.3	−1.3	6.0	0.0
Sri Lanka	4.2	5.0	+0.8	6.0	+1.8
East Asia					
China (Taiwan)	9.4	7.0	−2.4	8.0	−1.4
Indonesia	5.3	3.0	−2.3	4.0	−1.3
Korea, Republic of	10.1	5.0	−5.1	6.0	−3.9
Malaysia	6.5	5.0	−1.5	6.0	0.5
Philippines	5.6	5.5	0.1	6.0	0.4
Thailand	7.7	6.0	−1.7	6.5	−1.2
Middle East					
Iran	10.8	5.5	−5.3	6.5	−4.3
Israel	8.3	9.0	+0.7	10.0	+1.7
Jordan	2.9	5.6	+2.7	8.0	+5.1
Latin America					
Argentina	4.5	4.3	0.2	5.5	+1.0
Bolivia	5.1	4.5	−0.6	5.6	0.5
Brazil	7.8	5.5	−2.3	7.0	−0.8
Chile	3.0	5.0	+2.0	5.5	+2.5
Colombia	5.8	6.1	0.3	7.0	+1.2
Costa Rica	6.3	6.0	0.3	6.9	+0.6
Ecuador	6.4	5.0	−1.4	5.5	−0.9
El Salvador	4.9	6.0	+1.1	6.5	+1.6

Table A5 (*continued*)

Country	Annual GNP growth rates, 1962–75 [a]				
	Actual (1)	Chenery-Strout plan estimate [b] (2)	Error [c] (3)	Chenery-Strout upper limit estimate [d] (4)	Error [c] (5)
Guatemala	5.9	5.0	−0.9	5.5	0.4
Guyana	4.4	4.0	0.4	5.0	+0.6
Honduras	4.1	4.5	0.4	5.0	+0.9
Jamaica	5.7	4.5	−1.2	5.5	0.2
Mexico	6.6	6.0	−0.6	7.0	0.4
Nicaragua	5.0	5.0	0.0	5.5	0.5
Panama	6.7	5.0	−1.7	6.0	−0.7
Paraguay	5.0	3.0	−2.0	4.0	−1.0
Peru	4.7	5.5	+0.8	7.0	+2.3
Trinidad and Tobago	3.5	6.0	+1.5	8.8	+5.3
Venezuela	5.7	6.0	0.3	7.0	+1.3
Developing countries	c6.6	c5.2		c6.0	

Sources: Column 1: Data tapes, *World Bank Atlas* (1977). Columns 2 and 4: Chenery and Strout (1966), pp. 712–13.

a. Constant prices. The estimates refer to GNP, not GNP per capita.

b. Plan estimates are based on the development plans of the major countries, and are defined as those targets "achievable with moderate improvements in development policies in relation to past experience." (Chenery and Strout, 1966, p. 711.)

c. + = projection too high; − = projection too low; no sign: projection "correct," that is, up to 0.5 percentage points above or below the actual growth rate. The results may be summarized as follows:

Region	Number of times projection is			
	Too high (+)	Correct (0)	Too low (−)	Total
Chenery-Strout plan estimates				
Africa	3	5	5	13
South Asia	3	0	1	4
East Asia	0	1	5	6
Middle East	2	0	1	3
Latin America	4	7	8	19
Developing countries	12	13	20	45
Chenery-Strout upper limit estimates				
Africa	5	3	5	13
South Asia	3	1	0	4
East Asia	0	2	4	6
Middle East	2	0	1	3
Latin America	10	5	4	19
Developing countries	20	11	14	45

d. "Our notion of the upper limit implies a probability of perhaps one in four that the given growth target and performance could be attained" (Chenery and Strout, 1966, p. 714).

Table A6. Growth of Population, by Region and Country, 1950–75

Region and country	Population (thousands)		Annual growth rate (percent)			
	1950	1975	1950–60	1960–70	1970–75	1950–75
Africa	208,581	384,491	2.2	2.5	2.6	2.4
Algeria	8,190	15,747	2.1	3.2	3.2	2.6
Angola	4,258	5,470	1.6	1.3	0.1	1.0
Benin, People's Republic of	1,538	3,108	3.1	2.7	2.7	2.8
Botswana	411	665	2.0	1.9	1.9	1.9
Burundi	2,244	3,732	2.1	2.0	2.1	2.0
Cameroon	3,830	7,260	2.2	2.0	2.0	2.6
Central African Empire	1,057	1,787	2.0	2.2	2.2	2.1
Chad	2,647	4,035	1.5	1.7	2.1	1.6
Congo, People's Republic of	702	1,329	1.9	2.6	2.1	2.5
Egypt, Arab Republic of	20,461	37,096	2.4	2.6	2.2	2.4
Ethiopia	17,068	27,921	1.6	2.0	2.5	1.9
Gabon	416	536	0.7	1.0	1.7	1.0
Gambia, The	319	519	1.5	2.2	2.4	1.9
Ghana	5,385	9,869	2.2	2.6	2.7	2.4
Guinea	2,269	5,540	3.1	2.8	2.8	3.6
Ivory Coast	2,517	6,700	3.7	3.4	4.2	3.9
Kenya	6,176	13,349	3.0	3.1	3.5	3.1
Lesotho	614	1,217	2.1	2.2	2.2	2.7
Liberia	688	1,549	3.3	3.3	3.3	3.3
Libyan Arab Republic	939	2,442	3.7	3.7	5.0	3.8
Madagascar	4,354	8,835	2.4	2.6	3.1	2.9
Malawi	2,785	5,087	2.2	2.6	2.6	2.4
Mali	3,363	5,677	1.9	2.1	2.4	2.1
Mauritania	895	1,322	0.8	1.8	2.7	1.5
Mauritius	479	882	3.3	2.4	1.1	2.4
Morocco	8,953	16,680	2.6	2.4	2.4	2.5
Mozambique	5,934	9,240	1.4	1.9	2.4	1.7
Niger	2,396	4,562	2.5	2.7	2.6	2.6
Nigeria	42,646	75,023	1.9	2.5	2.5	2.2
Rhodesia	2,670	6,310	3.7	3.3	3.5	3.4
Rwanda	1,979	4,136	2.9	3.6	2.3	2.9
Senegal	2,528	5,000	2.1	2.6	2.7	2.7
Sierra Leone	1,888	2,982	1.1	2.2	2.5	1.8
Somalia	1,826	3,180	2.0	2.4	2.4	2.2
Sudan	8,947	15,550	2.9	2.2	2.1	2.2
Swaziland	249	494	2.4	2.9	3.2	2.7
Tanzania	7,719	14,738	2.2	3.0	2.7	2.6
Togo	1,099	2,235	2.8	2.7	2.7	2.8
Tunisia	3,330	5,588	2.3	2.1	2.3	2.0
Uganda	5,859	11,555	2.5	2.7	3.3	2.7

Table A6 (*continued*)

Region and country	Population (thousands)		Annual growth rate (percent)			
	1950	1975	1950– 60	1960– 70	1970– 75	1950– 75
Upper Volta	3,366	5,900	2.6	2.1	1.7	2.2
Zaïre	11,154	24,721	2.3	2.7	2.7	3.2
Zambia	2,431	4,920	2.8	2.9	2.9	2.8
South Asia	*482,360*	*830,441*	*1.9*	*2.4*	*2.4*	*2.1*
Afghanistan	9,623	16,670	1.8	2.2	2.2	2.2
Bangladesh	—ᵃ	78,600	n.a.	2.8	2.0	n.a.
Burma	18,766	30,170	1.8	2.2	2.2	1.8
India	358,293	609,582	1.8	2.3	2.4	2.1
Nepal	8,000	12,590	1.5	1.8	2.7	1.8
Pakistan	—ᵃ	69,229	n.a.	2.9	3.0	n.a.
Sri Lanka	7,678	13,600	2.6	2.4	1.7	2.3
East Asia	*171,489*	*312,387*	*2.6*	*2.4*	*2.2*	*2.4*
British Solomon Islands	n.a.	190	2.6	2.7	2.9	n.a.
China (Taiwan)	7,619	16,000	3.4	3.1	2.0	2.9
Fiji	289	569	3.2	2.8	1.9	2.7
Hong Kong	1,907	4,367	4.9	2.5	1.9	3.3
Indonesia	77,207	131,610	2.1	1.9	2.6	2.1
Khmer Republic	4,074	n.a.	2.9	2.4	2.9	n.a.
Korea, Republic of	18,900	34,018	2.8	2.3	1.6	2.3
Lao People's Democratic Republic	1,810	3,345	2.6	2.4	2.5	2.4
Malaysia	6,105	12,030	2.9	2.6	3.0	2.7
Papua New Guinea	1,453	2,719	2.7	2.4	2.0	2.5
Philippines	20,275	42,500	3.0	3.0	2.9	2.9
Singapore	1,022	2,249	4.8	2.3	1.7	3.2
Thailand	19,814	41,870	3.0	3.1	2.9	3.0
Vietnam	11,014	20,920	2.5	2.6	2.7	2.5
Middle East	*34,015*	*81,182*	*3.0*	*3.0*	*3.2*	*3.0*
Bahrain	n.a.	260	n.a.	3.5	4.2	n.a.
Iran	16,276	33,996	2.8	3.1	3.2	2.9
Iraq	5,124	11,120	3.0	3.2	3.3	3.1
Israel	1,258	3,469	5.3	3.3	3.3	4.1
Jordan	1,292	2,709	2.8	3.3	3.2	2.9
Kuwait	100	980	10.8	10.2	5.5	9.5
Lebanon	1,650	3,164	2.5	2.5	3.0	2.6
Oman	n.a.	773	n.a.	3.0	3.2	n.a.
Qatar	n.a.	202	n.a.	8.4	5.9	n.a.
Saudi Arabia	5,100	8,296	2.0	1.7	2.4	1.9
Syrian Arab Republic	3,215	7,409	3.6	3.3	3.3	3.4
United Arab Emirates	n.a.	656	n.a.	10.5	19.8	n.a.
Yemen Arab Republic	n.a.	6,471	2.2	2.3	2.4	n.a.
Yemen People's Democratic Republic	n.a.	1,677	2.6	3.2	3.2	n.a.

Table A6 (*continued*)

Region and country	Population (thousands)		Annual growth rate (percent)			
	1950	1975	1950–60	1960–70	1970–75	1950–75
Latin America	*149,515*	*303,949*	*2.8*	*2.8*	*2.8*	*2.8*
Argentina	17,085	25,016	1.5	1.5	1.5	1.5
Barbados	211	245	0.9	0.2	0.7	0.6
Belize	n.a.	140	3.0	2.8	3.3	n.a.
Bolivia	3,019	5,613	2.4	2.6	2.6	2.5
Brazil	51,973	106,996	3.0	2.9	2.9	2.9
Chile	6,058	10,585	2.4	2.4	1.7	2.2
Colombia	11,330	23,767	3.3	2.9	3.0	2.9
Costa Rica	859	1,970	3.9	3.3	2.7	3.3
Dominican Republic	2,135	4,695	3.6	2.9	2.9	3.1
Ecuador	3,231	7,121	3.0	3.4	3.2	3.2
El Salvador	1,922	4,006	2.7	3.5	3.1	2.9
Guatemala	2,791	5,395	3.1	2.5	2.1	2.6
Guyana	423	810	3.0	2.4	2.4	2.6
Haiti	n.a.	4,583	1.5	1.6	1.6	n.a.
Honduras	1,372	2,889	3.0	2.7	2.7	3.0
Jamaica	1,421	2,042	1.3	1.7	1.8	1.4
Mexico	26,282	59,928	3.2	3.4	3.5	3.3
Netherlands Antilles	n.a.	242	1.7	1.4	1.7	n.a.
Nicaragua	1,133	2,094	2.9	2.7	2.7	2.4
Panama	795	1,667	2.9	3.1	3.1	2.9
Paraguay	1,397	2,553	2.2	2.6	2.7	2.4
Peru	8,216	15,387	2.1	2.9	2.9	2.5
Surinam	n.a.	362	3.7	3.1	−0.1	n.a.
Trinidad and Tobago	632	1,080	2.8	2.1	1.1	2.1
Uruguay	2,193	2,764	1.5	0.6	0.4	0.9
Venezuela	5,034	11,993	3.7	3.4	3.1	3.5
Southern Europe	*82,016*	*116,199*	*1.4*	*1.4*	*1.4*	*1.4*
Cyprus	494	625	1.5	1.1	0.1	0.9
Greece	7,554	9,101	1.0	0.6	0.7	0.7
Malta	312	330	0.5	−0.2	−0.3	0.2
Portugal	8,405	9,357	0.5	0.1	0.4	0.4
Spain	27,868	35,358	0.8	1.1	1.0	0.9
Turkey	21,037	40,098	2.7	2.5	2.4	2.6
Yugoslavia	16,346	21,330	1.2	1.0	0.9	1.0

Table A6 (*continued*)

Region and country	Population (thousands)		Annual growth rate (percent)			
	1950	*1975*	*1950– 60*	*1960– 70*	*1970– 75*	*1950– 75*
OPEC countries	(*165,000*)	*300,000*	*2.3*	*2.5*	(*2.7*)	(*2.4*)
OECD countries	*499,952*	*653,553*	*1.3*	*1.0*	*0.8*	*1.0*
Australia	8,179	13,500	2.3	2.0	1.5	2.0
Austria	6,935	7,520	0.2	0.5	0.4	0.3
Belgium ᵇ	8,639	9,800	0.6	0.6	0.3	0.5
Canada	13,737	22,830	2.7	1.8	1.4	2.0
Denmark	4,271	5,060	0.7	0.8	0.5	0.6
Finland	4,009	4,710	1.0	0.4	0.5	0.6
France	41,736	52,910	0.9	1.0	0.8	0.9
Germany, Federal Republic of	49,986	61,830	1.0	0.9	0.4	0.8
Iceland	143	223	2.1	1.6	1.8	1.7
Ireland	2,969	3,127	−0.5	0.4	1.2	0.2
Italy	46,769	55,810	0.7	0.7	0.8	0.7
Japan	82,900	110,950	1.3	1.0	1.2	1.1
Luxembourg	n.a.	363	0.6	0.8	1.5	n.a.
Netherlands, The	10,114	13,650	1.3	1.3	0.9	1.1
New Zealand	1,908	3,090	2.2	1.7	1.9	1.9
Norway	3,265	4,010	0.9	0.8	0.7	0.8
Sweden	7,014	8,200	0.6	0.7	0.4	0.6
Switzerland	4,694	6,400	1.3	1.3	0.8	1.2
United Kingdom	50,413	55,960	0.4	0.6	0.2	0.4
United States	152,271	213,610	1.7	1.2	0.8	1.3
South Africa	12,878	25,470	2.5	2.7	2.6	2.7
All developing countries	*1,045,960*	*1,912,450*	*2.4*	*2.4*	*2.4*	*2.4*

n.a. Not available.
a. Total population of Pakistan and Bangladesh in 1950 was 80 million.
b. 1950 population figure includes Luxembourg.
Sources: Computed from World Bank, *World Tables 1976*, and data tapes, *World Bank Atlas* (1977).

Table A7. The Relative Gap in GNP per Capita, by Region and Country, 1950–75 [a]

(Percent)

Region and country	1950	1960	1965	1970	1975
Africa	*7.1*	*6.7*	*6.0*	*5.7*	*5.9* [b]
Algeria	20.3	23.1 [b]	13.9	13.4	13.7 [b]
Angola	9.5	12.3 [b]	12.9 [b]	12.0	11.9 [c]
Benin, People's Republic of	n.a.	3.7	3.0	2.7	2.4
Botswana	5.9	4.7	4.8 [b]	5.0 [b]	5.7 [b]
Burundi	4.9	2.6	2.1	1.9	1.7
Cameroon	5.6	4.8	4.8 [b]	5.2 [b]	4.7
Central African Empire	8.5	6.6	5.2	4.6	4.0
Chad	n.a.	3.9	3.0	2.5	2.1
Congo, People's Republic of	12.7	9.5	8.0	8.1 [b]	8.8 [b]
Egypt, Arab Republic of	8.5	6.9	6.8	5.6	5.5
Ethiopia	2.4	2.3	2.2	2.0	1.8
Gabon	n.a.	29.4	28.9	30.1 [b]	39.3 [b,c]
Gambia, The	4.0	3.0	3.0	2.7	3.4 [b]
Ghana	14.9	13.3	11.1	9.0	8.2
Guinea	n.a.	3.3	2.9	2.4	2.3
Ivory Coast	11.9	8.8	9.4 [b]	9.1	8.8
Kenya	5.4	4.4	3.7	3.8 [b]	3.8 [b]
Lesotho	n.a.	2.3	2.4	2.4	3.1 [b,c]
Liberia	n.a.	9.6	7.1	7.8 [b]	7.2
Libyan Arab Republic	33.1	27.2	58.2 [b]	76.6 [b]	89.3 [b,c]
Madagascar	8.2	6.0	4.6	4.2	3.4
Malawi	2.9	2.5	2.2	2.1	2.6 [b]
Mali	2.8	2.3	2.0	1.8	1.7
Mauritania	8.4	4.8	6.0 [b]	5.6	5.5
Mauritius	24.2	13.0	12.5	9.3	10.2
Morocco	14.8	10.2	8.8	8.0	8.3 [b]
Mozambique	7.4	8.1 [b]	6.9	7.4 [b]	5.4
Niger	n.a.	4.5	4.3	2.9	2.3
Nigeria	6.3	5.7	5.0	5.1 [b]	5.5 [b]
Rhodesia	n.a.	12.6	10.3	9.3	9.5 [b]
Rwanda	5.0	3.1	1.9	2.0 [b]	1.5
Senegal	10.0	11.3 [b]	9.1	6.5	6.5
Sierra Leone	n.a.	n.a.	4.3	4.0	3.5
Somalia	1.6	3.2 [b]	2.2	1.9	1.8 [c]
Sudan	4.9	4.8	3.8	2.9	5.1 [b,c]
Swaziland	3.3	4.4 [b]	6.0 [b]	6.2 [b]	8.3 [b,c]
Tanzania	3.5	3.8 [b]	3.3	3.3	3.1
Togo	6.9	4.4	4.8 [b]	4.9 [b]	4.7
Tunisia	n.a.	n.a.	10.9	10.2	13.3 [b,c]
Uganda	8.2	6.5	5.9	5.6	4.4
Upper Volta	4.2	2.9	2.4	2.1	1.7

Table A7 (*continued*)

Region and country	1950	1960	1965	1970	1975
Zaïre	3.9	3.2	3.0	2.8	2.7
Zambia	13.0	12.6	12.4	10.9	9.5
South Asia	*3.6*	*3.5*	*3.0*	*2.8*	*2.5*
Afghanistan	3.7	3.3 [b]	2.6 [b]	2.2	2.3 [b]
Bangladesh	n.a.	3.2	2.9	2.5	2.0
Burma	2.4	2.7 [b]	2.5	2.0	1.9
India	4.0	3.7 [b]	3.2	2.9	2.6
Nepal	3.6	2.9	2.5	2.1	1.9
Pakistan	n.a.	2.7	2.7	2.8 [b]	2.5
Sri Lanka	3.8	3.2	2.8	2.7	2.6
East Asia	*5.5*	*5.8* [b]	*5.5*	*5.8* [b]	*6.5* [b, c]
British Solomon Islands	n.a.	8.0	7.0	6.0	5.9
China (Taiwan)	9.4	11.1 [b]	11.9 [b]	13.1 [b]	15.6 [b, c]
Fiji	24.0	17.2	13.9	14.4	16.1 [b]
Hong Kong	19.7	20.8 [b]	25.8 [b]	29.0 [b]	30.2 [b, c]
Indonesia	4.3	3.8 [b]	3.1	3.1 [b]	3.2 [b]
Khmer Republic	4.7	4.1 [b]	3.5	2.7	n.a.
Korea, Republic of	6.2	5.9 [b]	5.7	7.2 [b]	9.6 [b, c]
Lao People's Democratic Republic	2.6	1.8	1.4	1.4 [b]	n.a.
Malaysia	14.7	11.8	11.9 [b]	11.7	12.7 [b]
Papua New Guinea	9.6	8.4 [b]	8.5 [b]	8.3	7.9
Philippines	7.1	7.2 [b]	6.6	6.1	6.5 [b]
Singapore	n.a.	26.6	25.3	34.4 [b]	44.0 [b, c]
Thailand	5.6	5.3 [b]	5.3 [b]	5.7 [b]	6.1 [b, c]
Vietnam	6.0	5.3 [b]	5.0	3.9	3.1
Middle East	*(19.3)*	*21.3* [b]	*22.7* [b]	*24.2* [b]	*31.7* [b, c]
Bahrain	n.a.	n.a.	n.a.	n.a.	42.8
Iran	16.1	16.0 [b]	15.9	18.6 [b]	25.2 [b, c]
Iraq	11.9	16.8 [b]	17.0 [b]	15.2	22.5 [b, c]
Israel	45.8	52.6 [b]	57.4 [b]	59.9 [b]	62.7 [b, c]
Jordan	7.8	10.4 [b]	12.7 [b]	9.3	8.1 [c]
Kuwait	805.6	495.8 [b]	372.9	258.4	202.2
Lebanon	29.0	21.9	20.3	18.7	n.a.
Oman	n.a.	8.9	8.1	15.5 [b]	36.3 [b, c]
Qatar	n.a.	119.3	82.2	88.7 [b]	146.1 [b, c]
Saudi Arabia	n.a.	24.2	29.4 [b]	33.4 [b]	52.8 [b, c]
Syrian Arab Republic	11.9	8.6	10.0 [b]	9.1	11.5 [b]
United Arab Emirates	n.a.	59.6	103.4 [b]	182.4 [b]	184.0 [b, c]
Yemen Arab Republic	n.a.	n.a.	n.a.	n.a.	n.a.
Yemen People's Democratic Republic	n.a.	n.a.	n.a.	5.4	4.3

Table A7 (*continued*)

Region and country	1950	1960	1965	1970	1975
Latin America	*20.8*	*19.0*	*17.6*	*16.9*	*18.0* [b]
Argentina	38.1	32.4	30.5	28.3	27.9
Barbados	16.9	19.9 [b]	20.3 [b]	23.9 [b]	22.0 [c]
Belize	17.8	16.4	14.9	13.6	13.4
Bolivia	10.3	6.1 [b]	5.8	5.2	5.5 [b]
Brazil	15.7	15.7	13.9	14.3	17.7 [c]
Chile	25.0	20.8	19.0	17.1	13.4
Colombia	13.0	10.9	9.6	9.1	9.7 [b]
Costa Rica	18.7	17.9	15.4	15.0	15.9 [b]
Dominican Republic	13.6	12.5	10.1	10.3 [b]	12.6 [b]
Ecuador	11.6	10.3	8.8	7.9	9.6 [b]
El Salvador	11.1	9.6 [b]	9.2	8.0	8.0 [b]
Guatemala	14.5	11.5	10.6	10.3	11.5 [b]
Guyana	16.1	13.5	11.5	10.4	9.8
Haiti	n.a.	5.0	3.9	3.2	3.1
Honduras	11.4	8.8	7.6	6.8	6.1
Jamaica	15.8	22.6 [b]	21.7	20.7	22.6 [b, c]
Mexico	23.6	22.1	21.6	21.0	21.0
Netherlands Antilles	80.5	53.2	38.3	32.7	30.5
Nicaragua	13.1	12.4 [b]	14.1 [b]	12.2	12.6 [b]
Panama	20.3	18.1 [b]	19.1	19.6	18.7
Paraguay	14.9	11.4	10.4	9.3	10.0 [b]
Peru	16.9	16.2 [b]	15.9	13.9	14.3 [b]
Surinam	n.a.	23.7	21.9	22.7 [b]	22.7
Trinidad and Tobago	30.0	39.6 [b]	35.0	31.9	33.3 [b, c]
Uruguay	41.1	35.3	28.5	25.8	23.3
Venezuela	41.7	43.5 [b]	41.5	38.5	39.0 [b]
Southern Europe	*(21.9)*	*28.5* [b]	*29.1* [b]	*26.7*	*30.2* [b, c]
Cyprus	26.8	24.4 [b]	25.4 [b]	27.9 [b]	20.7
Greece	23.4	27.6 [b]	32.6 [b]	37.1 [b]	41.5 [b, c]
Malta	17.3	16.7 [b]	14.7	18.4 [b]	23.9 [b, c]
Portugal	n.a.	n.a.	n.a.	n.a.	28.2
Romania	n.a.	23.5	24.2 [b]	23.9	29.5 [b, c]
Spain	29.9	36.9 [b]	38.7 [b]	40.7 [b]	47.5 [b, c]
Turkey	13.3	13.8 [b]	12.8	12.9 [b]	15.1 [b, c]
Yugoslavia	18.0	20.5 [b]	21.3 [b]	21.9 [b]	26.0 [b, c]
OPEC countries	*(11.2)*	*10.0*	*9.6*	*10.2* [b]	*12.4* [b, c]
Algeria	20.3	23.1 [b]	13.9	13.4	13.7 [b]
Ecuador	11.6	10.3	8.8	7.9	9.6 [b]
Gabon	n.a.	29.4	28.9	30.1 [b]	39.3 [b, c]
Indonesia	4.3	3.8	3.1	3.1 [b]	3.2 [b]

Table A7 (*continued*)

Region and country	1950	1960	1965	1970	1975
Iran	16.1	16.0	15.9	18.6 [b]	25.2 [b,c]
Iraq	11.9	16.8 [b]	17.0 [b]	15.2	22.5 [b,c]
Kuwait	805.6	495.8	372.9	258.4	202.2
Libyan Arab Republic	33.1	27.2	58.2 [b]	76.6 [b]	89.3 [b,c]
Nigeria	6.3	5.7	5.0	5.1 [b]	5.5 [b]
Qatar	n.a.	119.3	82.2	88.7 [b]	146.1 [b,c]
Saudi Arabia	n.a.	24.2	29.4 [b]	33.4 [b]	52.8 [b,c]
United Arab Emirates	n.a.	59.6	103.4 [b]	182.4 [b]	184.0 [b,c]
Venezuela	41.7	43.5 [b]	41.5	38.5	39.0 [b]
OECD countries	*100.0*	*100.0*	*100.0*	*100.0*	*100.0*
Australia	126.1	108.0	102.6	98.9	99.1 [b]
Austria	59.3	74.7 [b]	73.8	76.7 [b]	82.9 [b,c]
Belgium	101.1	94.7	96.5 [b]	99.2 [b]	106.5 [b,c]
Canada	141.9	118.0	115.6	111.5	116.7 [b]
Denmark	130.5	123.3	125.0 [b]	123.3	121.5
Finland	71.1	76.9 [b]	78.9 [b]	82.8 [b]	89.5 [b,c]
France	86.8	90.4 [b]	92.1 [b]	97.1 [b]	101.1 [b,c]
Germany, Federal Republic of	84.3	120.1 [b]	118.3	120.1 [b]	116.1 [c]
Iceland	116.1	110.8	114.4 [b]	96.6	98.7 [b]
Ireland	49.4	45.4	44.5	45.0 [b]	42.5
Italy	39.3	49.1 [b]	50.3 [b]	53.7 [b]	51.6 [c]
Japan	27.7	41.4 [b]	52.3 [b]	70.8 [b]	78.4 [b,c]
Luxembourg	148.9	130.2	119.7	115.6	106.3
Netherlands, The	97.2	98.3 [b]	95.7	98.0 [b]	98.2 [b,c]
New Zealand	128.4	102.7	96.2	86.4	82.2
Norway	113.4	108.2	111.0 [b]	107.5	114.9 [b,c]
Sweden	144.7	140.8	144.1 [b]	139.0	138.3
Switzerland	165.6	164.3	159.3	152.4	141.3
United Kingdom	86.8	81.2	75.6	68.2	67.4
United States	166.3	142.5	137.4	127.8	124.0
South Africa	29.3	25.6	24.5	23.5	23.1

a. Relative gap is GNP per capita of individual country or region as a percentage of average GNP per capita of the OECD countries.

b. Relative gap decreased in the five-year period (increased for countries above OECD average).

c. Relative gap decreased during 1950–75 (increased for countries above OECD average).

Sources: Computed from data tapes, *World Bank Atlas* (1977). GNP per capita for 1950 is estimated by applying the growth rate of GDP per capita in 1950–60 (*World Tables 1976*) to figures for GNP per capita in 1960 (*World Bank Atlas*).

Table A8. The Absolute Gap in GNP per Capita, by Region and Country, 1950–75 [a]
(1974 U.S. dollars)

Region and country	1950	1960	1965	1970	1975
Africa	*2,208*	*3,006*	*3,695*	*4,478*	*4,930*
Algeria	1,894	2,477	3,385	4,114	4,520
Angola	2,153	2,825	3,422	4,179	4,615
Benin, People's Republic of	n.a.	3,103	3,813	4,622	5,113
Botswana	2,238	3,069	3,743	4,512	4,938
Burundi	2,261	3,138	3,848	4,660	5,147
Cameroon	2,246	3,067	3,741	4,501	4,992
Central African Empire	2,177	3,009	3,724	4,529	5,026
Chad	n.a.	3,097	3,812	4,631	5,127
Congo, People's Republic of	2,075	2,917	3,617	4,366	4,778
Egypt, Arab Republic of	2,176	3,000	3,664	4,483	4,952
Ethiopia	2,321	3,149	3,844	4,657	5,144
Gabon	n.a.	2,273	2,792	3,319	3,177 [b]
Gambia, The	2,284	3,125	3,812	4,621	5,060
Ghana	2,025	2,794	3,492	4,323	4,811
Guinea	n.a.	3,114	3,816	4,637	5,120
Ivory Coast	2,096	2,938	3,560	4,317	4,778
Kenya	2,250	3,079	3,786	4,571	5,038
Lesotho	n.a.	3,148	3,835	4,637	5,077
Liberia	n.a.	2,913	3,650	4,380	4,861
Libyan Arab Republic	1,592	2,344	1,642 [b]	1,111 [b]	563 [b,c]
Madagascar	2,184	3,029	3,748	4,552	5,058
Malawi	2,310	3,141	3,843	4,649	5,101
Mali	2,312	3,146	3,850	4,666	5,151
Mauritania	2,178	3,068	3,695	4,486	4,950
Mauritius	1,804	2,802	3,437	4,306	4,705
Morocco	2,026	2,893	3,585	4,371	4,803
Mozambique	2,201	2,962	3,660	4,399	4,954
Niger	n.a.	3,077	3,759	4,610	5,116
Nigeria	2,229	3,037	3,732	4,507	4,951
Rhodesia	n.a.	2,814	3,524	4,307	4,739
Rwanda	2,260	3,122	3,854	4,653	5,157
Senegal	2,141	2,856	3,573	4,442	4,897
Sierra Leone	n.a.	3,221	3,759	4,558	5,057
Somalia	2,341	3,119	3,844	4,657	5,146
Sudan	2,261	3,068	3,780	4,611	4,971
Swaziland	2,299	3,080	3,693	4,454	4,804
Tanzania	2,294	3,100	3,800	4,593	5,078
Togo	2,215	3,079	3,743	4,519	4,993
Tunisia	n.a.	3,221	3,503	4,266	4,543
Uganda	2,184	3,011	3,699	4,483	5,009

Table A8 (*continued*)

Region and country	1950	1960	1965	1970	1975
Upper Volta	2,279	3,129	3,836	4,649	5,151
Zaïre	2,285	3,117	3,813	4,615	5,099
Zambia	2,069	2,817	3,442	4,230	4,743
South Asia	*2,293*	*3,109*	*3,810*	*4,616*	*5,106*
Afghanistan	2,290	3,115	3,826	4,644	5,119
Bangladesh	n.a.	3,117	3,815	4,631	5,135
Burma	2,322	3,133	3,832	4,654	5,138
India	2,284	3,103	3,805	4,610	5,099
Nepal	2,292	3,126	3,832	4,648	5,136
Pakistan	n.a.	3,135	3,825	4,619	5,107
Sri Lanka	2,288	3,118	3,819	4,621	5,104
East Asia	*2,248*	*3,035*	*3,712*	*4,475*	*4,897*
British Solomon Islands	n.a.	2,964	3,654	4,466	4,931
China (Taiwan)	2,154	2,863	3,463	4,127	4,421
Fiji	1,808	2,666	3,383	4,068	4,396
Hong Kong	1,909	2,552	2,915	3,371	3,654
Indonesia	2,275	3,100	3,809	4,603	5,069
Khmer Republic	2,266	3,089	3,790	4,619	5,238
Korea, Republic of	2,232	3,032	3,704	4,406	4,734
Lao People's Democratic Republic	2,316	3,162	3,873	4,681	5,238
Malaysia	2,028	2,842	3,462	4,195	4,573
Papua New Guinea	2,150	2,950	3,596	4,357	4,826
Philippines	2,210	2,991	3,672	4,461	4,898
Singapore	n.a.	2,365	2,937	3,115	2,931 [b]
Thailand	2,246	3,050	3,722	4,481	4,919
Vietnam	2,235	3,052	3,734	4,562	5,075
Middle East	*(1,918)*	*2,535*	*3,037*	*3,599*	*3,578*
Bahrain	n.a.	n.a.	n.a.	n.a.	2,994
Iran	1,995	2,705	3,305	3,868	3,917
Iraq	2,095	2,679	3,261	4,026	4,058
Israel	1,288	1,528	1,673	1,903	1,951
Jordan	2,193	2,886	3,430	4,308	4,815
Kuwait	−16,781	−12,748	−10,724	−7,522	−5,352
Lebanon	1,688	2,517	3,131	3,860	n.a.
Oman	n.a.	2,934	3,613	4,013	3,335 [b]
Qatar	n.a.	−623	700	538 [b]	−2,417 [b]
Saudi Arabia	n.a.	2,441	2,774	3,164	2,471 [b]
Syrian Arab Republic	2,096	2,944	3,535	4,316	4,634
United Arab Emirates	n.a.	1,309	−133 [b]	−3,915 [b]	−4,397 [b]
Yemen Arab Republic	n.a.	n.a.	n.a.	n.a.	n.a.
Yemen People's Democratic Republic	n.a.	n.a.	3,930	4,494	5,014

Table A8 (*continued*)

Region and country	1950	1960	1965	1970	1975
Latin America	*1,883*	*2,609*	*3,240*	*3,948*	*4,294*
Argentina	1,471	2,179	2,731	3,403	3,774
Barbados	1,977	2,579	3,134	3,612	4,083
Belize	1,955	2,695	3,345	4,103	4,538
Bolivia	2,134	3,024	3,702	4,502	4,948
Brazil	2,006	2,715	3,382	4,069	4,311
Chile	1,783	2,550	3,182	3,939	4,538
Colombia	2,070	2,871	3,554	4,318	4,728
Costa Rica	1,933	2,646	3,324	4,037	4,404
Dominican Republic	2,054	2,818	3,532	4,261	4,577
Ecuador	2,103	2,888	3,583	4,373	4,735
El Salvador	2,116	2,913	3,567	4,371	4,820
Guatemala	2,033	2,851	3,515	4,260	4,636
Guyana	1,996	2,786	3,477	4,256	4,726
Haiti	n.a.	3,059	3,775	4,599	5,075
Honduras	2,107	2,938	3,629	4,425	4,916
Jamaica	2,002	2,494	3,077	3,767	4,053
Mexico	1,816	2,509	3,081	3,754	4,146
Netherlands Antilles	465	1,509	2,423	3,198	3,643
Nicaragua	2,066	2,821	3,377	4,168	4,577
Panama	1,895	2,637	3,181	3,820	4,261
Paraguay	2,025	2,853	3,520	4,308	4,713
Peru	1,975	2,700	3,303	4,090	4,490
Surinam	n.a.	2,457	3,069	3,670	4,051
Trinidad and Tobago	1,665	1,944	2,555	3,235	3,492
Uruguay	1,401	2,084	2,811	3,525	4,018
Venezuela	1,386	1,822	2,298	2,921	3,193
Southern Europe	*(1,858)*	*2,502*	*2,986*	*3,482*	*3,658*
Cyprus	1,741	2,436	2,931	3,422	4,156
Greece	1,822	2,332	2,650	2,988	3,065
Malta	1,967	2,684	3,352	3,877	3,988
Portugal	n.a.	n.a.	n.a.	n.a.	3,759
Romania	n.a.	2,464	2,979	3,617	3,695
Spain	1,668	2,031	2,410	2,815	2,751 [b]
Turkey	2,063	2,776	3,427	4,137	4,445
Yugoslavia	1,949	2,561	3,094	3,709	3,874

Table A8 (*continued*)

Region and country	1950	1960	1965	1970	1975
OPEC countries	*(2,178)*	*2,898*	*3,552*	*4,264*	*4,590*
OECD countries	*0*	*0*	*0*	*0*	*0*
Australia	−620	−258	−102	54	48 [b]
Austria	969	814 [b]	1,031	1,107	895 [b,c]
Belgium	−27	172	137 [b]	37	−340 [b,c]
Canada	−996	−580	−615 [b]	−548	−874 [b]
Denmark	−725	−752 [b]	−982 [b]	−1,106 [b]	−1,128 [b,c]
Finland	688	743	828	816 [b]	552 [b,c]
France	315	310 [b]	310 [b]	138 [b]	−57 [b,c]
Germany, Federal Republic of	374	−649 [b]	−718 [b]	−954 [b]	−842 [c]
Iceland	−384	−349	−564 [b]	161	66 [b]
Ireland	1,203	1,760	2,180	2,611	3,013
Italy	1,444	1,640	1,952	2,200	2,534
Japan	1,720	1,888	1,876 [b]	1,388 [b]	1,133 [b,c]
Luxembourg	−1,164	−972	−775	−741	−330
Netherlands, The	67	53 [b]	170	97 [b]	95 [b]
New Zealand	−676	−86	148	644	935
Norway	318	−264 [b]	−431 [b]	−356	−781 [b,c]
Sweden	−1,063	−1,315 [b]	−1,732 [b]	−1,855 [b]	−2,005 [b,c]
Switzerland	1,559	−2,071 [b]	−2,332 [b]	−2,489 [b]	−2,163 [c]
United Kingdom	315	605	958	1,509	1,706
United States	−1,576	−1,368	−1,471 [b]	−1,319	−1,258
South Africa	1,682	2,397	2,966	3,635	4,027

n.a. Not available.

a. Absolute gap is average GNP per capita of the OECD countries less GNP per capita of the individual country or region.

b. Absolute gap decreased in the five-year period (increased for countries above the OECD average).

c. Absolute gap decreased 1950–75 (increased for countries above the OECD average).

Source: Same as Table A7.

References

Abramovitz, Moses. 1975. "Economic Growth and Its Discontents." Stanford, Calif.: Stanford University. Processed.

Adelman, Irma. 1975. "Development Economics—A Reassessment of Goals." *The American Economic Review,* vol. 65, no. 2 (May), pp. 302–09.

————. 1975a. "Growth, Income Distribution and Equity-Oriented Development Strategies." *World Development,* vol. 3, no. 2 (February), pp. 67–76.

————, and Cynthia Taft Morris. 1973. *Economic Growth and Social Equity in Developing Countries.* Stanford, Calif.: Stanford University Press.

————, and Cynthia Taft Morris. 1975. "Distribution and Development: A Comment." *Journal of Development Economics,* vol. 1, no. 4 (February), pp. 401–02.

————, and Cynthia Taft Morris. 1977. "Growth and Impoverishment in the Middle of the Nineteenth Century." Paper read at the World Bank Workshop on Analysis of Distributional Issues in Development Planning, April 22–27 at Bellagio, Italy. Processed.

————, Cynthia Taft Morris, and Sherman Robinson. 1976. "Policies for Equitable Growth." *World Development,* vol. 4, no. 7 (July), pp. 561–82.

————, and others. 1977. "A Comparison of Two Models for Income Distribution Planning." Paper read at the World Bank Workshop on Analysis of Distributional Issues in Development Planning, April 22–27 at Bellagio, Italy. Processed.

————, and Sherman Robinson. 1977. *Income Distribution Policy in Developing Countries.* Stanford, Calif.: Stanford University Press.

Adler, John H. 1972. "The World Bank's Concept of Development— An In-House *Dogmengeschichte.*" In *Development and Planning: Essays in Honor of Paul Rosenstein-Rodan.* Edited by Jagdish Bhagwati and Richard Eckaus. London: George Allen and Unwin.

Ahluwalia, Montek. 1974. "Income Inequality: Some Dimensions

105

of the Problem." In *Redistribution with Growth*. By Hollis Chenery and others. London: Oxford University Press.

————. 1976. "Inequality, Poverty, and Development." *Journal of Development Economics*, vol. 3, no. 3 (December), pp. 307–42.

————. 1977. "Rural Poverty and Agricultural Growth in India." Washington, D.C.: World Bank. Processed.

————, and John Duloy. 1976. "Comments" (on Adelman, Morris, and Robinson, 1976). Washington, D.C.: World Bank. Processed.

————, and John Duloy. 1977. "Poverty Alleviation and Growth Pessimism: A Re-examination of Cross-Country Evidence." Paper read at the World Bank Workshop on Analysis of Distributional Issues in Development Planning, April 22–27 at Bellagio, Italy. Processed.

Amin, Samir. 1974. "Accumulation and Development: A Theoretical Model." *Review of African Political Economy*, no. 1 (August–November), pp. 9–26.

————. 1974a. *Accumulation on a World Scale*. New York: Monthly Review Press.

Anderson, C. A., and M. J. Bowman. 1965. *Education and Economic Development*. Chicago: Aldine.

Arndt, H. W. 1972. "Development Economics before 1945." In *Development and Planning: Essays in Honour of Paul Rosenstein-Rodan*. Edited by Jadish Bhagwati and Richard Eckaus. Amsterdam: North-Holland.

————. 1975. "Development and Equality: The Indonesian Case." *World Development*, vol. 3, no. 2 (February), pp. 77–90.

Atkinson, A. B. 1975. *The Economics of Inequality*. London: Oxford University Press.

Avramovic, Dragoslav. 1958. *Postwar Growth in International Indebtedness*. Baltimore: Johns Hopkins Press.

————, and Ravi Gulhati. 1960. *Debt Servicing Problems of Low-Income Countries, 1956–1958*. Baltimore: Johns Hopkins Press.

Bacha, Edmar. 1976. "On Some Contributions to the Brazilian Income Distribution Debate—I." Harvard Institute for International Development Discussion Paper, no. 11. Cambridge, Mass.

————. 1977. "The Kuznets Curve and Beyond: Growth and Changes in Inequalities." Paper read at the World Bank Workshop on Analysis of Distributional Issues in Development Planning, April 22–27 at Bellagio, Italy. Processed.

————, and Lance Taylor. 1977. "Brazilian Income Distribution in the 1960s: 'Facts,' Model Results, and the Controversy." Paper read at the World Bank Workshop on Analysis of Distributional Issues in Development Planning, April 22–27 at Bellagio, Italy. Processed.

Balassa, Bela. 1964. "The Capital Needs of the Developing Countries." *Kyklos,* vol. 17, no. 2, pp. 197–206.

————. 1964a. "The Purchasing Power Parity Doctrine: A Reappraisal." *Journal of Political Economy,* vol. 72, no. 6 (December), pp. 584–96.

————. 1971. "Industrial Policies in Taiwan and Korea." *Weltwirtschaftliches Archiv,* vol. 106, no. 1, pp. 55–77.

————. 1973. "Just How Misleading Are Official Exchange Rate Conversions? A Comment." *Economic Journal,* vol. 83, no. 332 (December), pp. 1258–67.

————. 1977. "Export Incentives and Export Performance in Developing Countries: A Comparative Analysis." World Bank Staff Working Paper no. 248. Washington, D.C.: World Bank. Processed.

————, and others. 1971. *The Structure of Protection in Developing Countries.* Baltimore: Johns Hopkins Press.

Baran, Paul. 1952. "On the Political Economy of Backwardness." *The Manchester School of Economic and Social Studies,* vol. 20, no. 1 (January), pp. 66–84.

Bardhan, Pranab. 1967. "Optimum Foreign Borrowing." In *Essays on the Theory of Optimal Economic Growth.* Edited by Karl Shell. Cambridge, Mass.: M.I.T. Press.

————. 1970. *Economic Growth, Development, and Foreign Trade: A Study in Pure Theory.* New York: John Wiley.

Barlow, Robin. 1977. "A Test of Alternative Methods of Making GNP Comparisons." *Economic Journal,* vol. 87, no. 347 (September), pp. 450–59.

Baster, Nancy. 1972. "Development Indicators: An Introduction." *Journal of Development Studies,* vol. 8, no. 3 (April), pp. 1–20.

Baumol, William. 1968. "Entrepreneurship in Economic Theory." *American Economic Review,* vol. 58, no. 2 (May), pp. 64–71.

Berg, Alan. 1973. *The Nutrition Factor.* Washington, D.C.: Brookings Institution.

Bernstein, Henry, ed. 1974. *Underdevelopment and Development.* Baltimore: Penguin.

Berry, Albert. 1972. "Unemployment as a Social Welfare Problem in Urban Colombia: Some Preliminary Hypotheses and Conclusions." Yale University Economic Growth Center Discussion Paper, no. 145. New Haven, Conn.

————, and Miguel Urrutia. 1976. *Income Distribution in Colombia.* New Haven: Yale University Press.

Bhagwati, Jagdish. 1966. *The Economics of Underdeveloped Countries.* New York: McGraw-Hill.

————. 1972. "The Key Issues." In *Economics and World Order: From the 1970s to the 1990s.* Edited by Jagdish Bhagwati. London: Macmillan.

————, ed. 1972a. *Economics and World Order: From the 1970s to the 1990s.* London: Macmillan.

————, ed. 1976. *The Brain Drain and Taxation: Theory and Empirical Analysis.* Amsterdam: North-Holland.

————. 1978. *Foreign Trade Regimes and Economic Growth: Liberalization Attempts and Consequences.* New York: Ballinger, for the National Bureau of Economic Research.

————, and Richard Eckaus, eds. 1972. *Development and Planning: Essays in Honour of Paul Rosenstein-Rodan.* London: George Allen and Unwin.

————, and Bent Hansen. 1972. "Should Growth Rates Be Evaluated at International Prices." In *Development and Planning: Essays in Honor of Paul Rosenstein-Rodan.* Edited by Jagdish Bhagwati and Richard Eckaus. London: George Allen and Unwin.

————, and M. Partington, eds. 1976. *Taxing the Brain Drain: A Proposal.* Amsterdam: North-Holland.

Bird, R. M., and L. H. De Wulf. 1973. "Taxation and Income Distribution in Latin America: A Critcial Review of Empirical Studies." *International Monetary Fund Staff Papers,* vol. 19, no. 3 (November), pp. 639–82.

Bowley, A. L. 1923. *The Nature and Purpose of the Measurement of Social Phenomena.* London: Macmillan.

Britnell, G. E. 1953. "Factors in the Economic Development of Guatemala." *American Economic Review,* vol. 43, no. 2 (May), pp. 104–14.

Bruno, Michael. 1977. "Distributional Issues in Development Planning—Some Reflections on the State of the Art." Paper read at the World Bank Workshop on Analysis of Distributional Issues in Development Planning, April 22–27 at Bellagio, Italy. Processed.

Bruton, Henry. 1973. "Economic Development and Labor Use: A Review." *World Development*, vol. 1, no. 12 (December), pp. 1–22.

Burki, Shahid Javed, and Joris Voorhoeve. 1977. "Global Estimates for Meeting Basic Needs: Background Paper." Washington, D.C.: World Bank. Processed.

Byers, T. J., ed. 1972. *Foreign Resources and Economic Development: A Symposium on the Report of the Pearson Commission.* London: Frank Cass.

Cantril, Hadley. 1965. *The Pattern of Human Concerns.* New Brunswick, N.J.: Rutgers University Press.

Carnoy, Martin, and Jorge Wertheim. 1976. "Cuba: Economic Change and Educational Reform, 1955–1974." Washington, D.C.: World Bank. Processed.

Cassel, Gustav. 1918. "Abnormal Deviations in International Exchanges." *Economic Journal,* vol. 28, no. 4 (December), pp. 413–15.

Cassen, Robert. 1976. "Population and Development: A Survey." *World Development*, vol. 4, no. 10 (October), pp. 785–830.

Chenery, Hollis. 1975. "The Structuralist Approach to Development Policy." *American Economic Review,* vol. 65, no. 2 (May), pp. 310–16.

———. 1976. "Transitional Growth and World Industrialization." Paper presented at the Nobel Symposium on the International Allocation of Economic Activity. Stockholm. Processed.

———, and Nicholas Carter. 1973. "Foreign Assistance and Development Performance." *American Economic Review,* vol. 63, no. 2 (May), pp. 459–68.

———, and Nicholas Carter. 1973a. "Internal and External Aspects of Development Plans and Performance, 1960–70." World Bank Development Policy Staff Working Paper, no. 141. Washington, D.C.: World Bank. Processed.

———, Hazel Elkington and Christopher Sims. 1970. "A Uniform Analysis of Development Patterns." Economic Development Report no. 148. Cambridge, Mass.: Harvard University Center for International Affairs. Processed.

————, and others. 1974. *Redistribution with Growth*. London: Oxford University Press.

————, and Alan Strout. 1966. "Foreign Assistance and Economic Development." *American Economic Review,* vol. 56, no. 4/1 (September), pp. 679–733.

————, and Moises Syrquin. 1975. *Patterns of Development, 1950– 1970*. London: Oxford University Press.

Clague, Christopher, and Vito Tanzi. 1972. "Human Capital, Natural Resources, and the Purchasing Power Parity Doctrine: Some Empirical Results." *Economia Internazionale,* vol. 25, no. 1 (February), pp. 3–18.

Cline, William. 1975. "Distribution and Development: A Survey of Literature." *Journal of Development Economics,* vol. 1, no. 4 (February), pp. 359–400.

————. n.d. "Policy Instruments for Rural Income Redistribution." Washington, D.C.: Brookings Institution. Processed.

Coombs, Philip, with Manzoor Ahmed. 1974. *Attacking Rural Poverty: How Non-Formal Education Can Help*. Baltimore: Johns Hopkins University Press.

Daly, D. J., ed. 1972. *International Comparisons of Prices and Output*. Conference on Research in Income and Wealth, Studies in Income and Wealth, volume 37. New York: National Bureau of Economic Research.

David, Paul, and Melvin Reder, eds. 1974. *Nations and Households in Economic Growth: Essays in Honor of Moses Abramovitz*. New York: Academic Press.

Díaz-Alejandro, Carlos. 1973. "Trade Policies and Economic Development." Yale University Economic Growth Center Discussion Paper, no. 180. New Haven.

————. 1975. "Data Needs in Development Economics." Yale University Economic Growth Center Discussion Paper, no. 232. New Haven.

Easterlin, Richard. 1974. "Does Economic Growth Improve The Human Lot?" In *Nations and Households in Economic Growth: Essays in Honor of Moses Abramovitz*. Edited by David Paul and Melvin Reder. New York: Academic Press.

Edwards, Edgar. 1974. "Employment in Developing Countries." *World Development,* vol. 2, no. 7 (July), pp. 1–28.

————, and Michael Todaro. 1974. "Education, Society and Development: Some Main Themes and Suggested Strategies for International Assistance." *World Development,* vol. 2, no. 1 (January), pp. 25–30.

Ellsworth, P. T. 1953. "Factors in the Economic Development of Ceylon." *American Economic Review,* vol. 43, no. 2 (May), pp. 115–25.

Emmerson, Donald. 1977. "Introducing Technology: The Need to Consider Local Culture." *International Development Review/ Focus,* vol. 19, no. 1 (June), pp. 17–20.

Enos, J. L. 1976. "Thoughts Upon Reading *Redistribution with Growth.*" Oxford: Magdalen College. Processed.

Epstein, T. Scarlett. 1970. "Indigenous Entrepreneurs and their Narrow Horizon." *New Guinea Research Bulletin,* no. 35. Boroko and Canberra.

Fei, John, and Gustav Ranis. 1975. "A Model of Growth and Employment in the Open Dualistic Economy: The Cases of Korea and Taiwan." *Journal of Development Studies,* vol. 11, no. 2 (January), pp. 32–63.

———, and Shirley Kuo. 1976. "Equity with Growth: the Taiwan Case." New Haven: Yale University Economic Growth Center. Processed.

Felix, David. 1976. "Economic Growth and Income Distribution in Mexico." St. Louis: Washington University. Processed.

Ffrench-Davis, Ricardo. 1977. "The Andean Pact: A Model of Economic Integration for Developing Countries." *World Development,* vol. 5, no. 1 (January), pp. 137–53.

Fields, Gary. 1977. "Poverty, Inequality, and Development: Alleviation or Exacerbation?" Paper read at the CEDE Conference on Distribution, Poverty, and Development, Universidad de Los Andes, June 6–9 at Bogotá, Colombia. Processed.

Fishlow, Albert. 1972. "Brazilian Size Distribution of Income." *American Economic Review,* vol. 62, no. 2 (May), pp. 391–402.

———. 1973. "Brazilian Income Size Distribution—Another Look." Berkeley, Calif.: University of California. Processed.

———. 1977. "Brazilian Income Distribution: Does Trickle-Down Really Work?" Paper read at the World Bank Workshop on Analysis of Distributional Issues in Development Planning, April 22–27 at Bellagio, Italy. Processed.

Food and Agriculture Organization. 1975. *The State of Food and Agriculture 1974.* Rome.

Foster, Philip. 1965. "The Vocational School Fallacy in Development Planning." In *Education and Economic Development.* Edited by C. A. Anderson and M. J. Bowman. Chicago: Aldine.

Foxley, Alejandro. 1976. *Income Distribution in Latin America.* Cambridge: Cambridge University Press.

Frank, André Gunder. 1969. *Capitalism and Underdevelopment in Latin America: Historical Studies of Chile and Brazil.* New York: Monthly Review Press.

———. 1969a. *Underdevelopment or Revolution: Essays on the Development of Underdevelopment and the Immediate Enemy.* New York: Monthly Review Press.

Frank, André Gunder. 1977. "Dependence Is Dead, Long Live Dependence and the Class Struggle: An Answer to Critics." *World Development,* vol. 5, no. 4 (April), pp. 355–70.

Furtado, Celso. 1963. *The Economic Growth of Brazil.* Berkeley: University of California Press.

———. 1967. *Development and Underdevelopment.* Berkeley: University of California Press.

———. 1973. "The Concept of External Dependence in the Study of Underdevelopment." In *The Political Economy of Development and Underdevelopment.* Edited by C. Wilber. New York: Random.

Gerschenkron, Alexander. 1962. *Economic Backwardness in Historical Perspective.* Cambridge, Mass.: Harvard University Press.

Gilbert, Milton, and Irving Kravis. 1954. *An International Comparison of National Products and the Purchasing Power of Currencies: A Study of the United States, the United Kingdom, France, Germany, and Italy.* Paris: Organisation for European Economic Cooperation.

Government of India, Planning Commission. 1952. *The First Five Year Plan: A Summary.* New Delhi.

Grant, James. 1976. "A Fresh Approach to Meeting Basic Human Needs of the World's Poorest Billion: Implications of the Chinese and Other Success Models." Washington, D.C.: Overseas Development Council. Processed.

Green, Reginald, and Ann Seidman. 1968. *Unity or Poverty? The Economics of Pan-Africanism.* Baltimore: Penguin.

Griffin, Keith. 1976. *Land Concentration and Rural Poverty.* New York: Holmes and Meier.

―――. 1977. "Increasing Poverty and Changing Ideas About Development Strategies." Paper read at the CEDE Conference on Distribution, Poverty, and Development, Universidad de Los Andes, June 6–9 at Bogotá, Colombia. Processed.

―――, and Azizur Khan. 1977. "Poverty in the Third World: Ugly Facts and Fancy Models." *World Development* (forthcoming).

―――, eds. 1977. *Poverty and Landlessness in Rural Asia.* Geneva: International Labour Office. Processed.

Grimes, Orville F., Jr. 1976. *Housing for Low Income Urban Families: Economics and Policy in the Developing World.* Baltimore: Johns Hopkins University Press.

Guisinger, Stephen. 1977. "Factor Prices in Pakistan." Washington, D.C.: World Bank. Processed.

―――, and Mohammed Irfan. 1974. "Real Wages of Industrial Workers in Pakistan: 1954 to 1970." *Pakistan Development Review,* vol. 13, no. 4 (Winter), pp. 363–88.

Gupta, S. 1975. "Income Distribution, Employment, and Growth: A Case Study of Indonesia." World Bank Staff Working Paper, no. 212. Washington, D.C.: World Bank.

Haberler, Gottfried. 1961. *A Survey of International Trade Theory.* Special Papers in International Economics, no. 1. Princeton: Princeton University.

Hagen, E. E. 1962. *On the Theory of Social Change.* Homewood, Ill.: Dorsey.

Hamada, K. 1965. "Optimum Capital Accumulation of an Economy Facing an International Capital Market: The Case of an Imperfect World Capital Market." University of Chicago Economics Department Technical Report, no. 4. Chicago.

Haq, Mahbub ul. 1971. "Employment in the 1970's: A New Perspective." *International Development Review,* no. 4. Reprinted in *The Poverty Curtain.* By Mahbub ul Haq. New York: Columbia University Press. 1976.

―――. 1976. "Concessions or Structural Change." Paper presented at A Special Meeting of the Club of Rome on the New International Order.

―――. 1976a. *The Poverty Curtain.* New York: Columbia University Press.

————. 1977. "Basic Needs: A Progress Report." Washington, D.C.: World Bank. Processed.

Harris, John. 1970. "Some Problems in Identifying the Role of Entrepreneurship in Economic Development: The Nigerian Case." *Explorations in Economic History,* vol. 7, no. 3 (Spring), pp. 347–69.

Hartwell, R. M. 1972. "The Consequences of the Industrial Revolution in England for the Poor." In *The Long Debate on Poverty.* By R. M. Hartwell and others. London: Institute of Economic Affairs.

————, and others. 1972. *The Long Debate on Poverty.* London: Institute of Economic Affairs.

Herrera, Amilcar, and others. 1976. *Catastrophe or New Society? A Latin American World Model* (The Bariloche Model). Ottawa: International Development Research Center.

Higgins, Benjamin. 1959. *Economic Development.* London: Constable.

Hill, Polly. 1970. *Studies in Rural Capitalism in West Africa.* Cambridge: Cambridge University Press.

Hirschman, Albert. 1971. *A Bias for Hope.* New Haven: Yale University Press.

————. 1973. "The Changing Tolerance for Income Inequality in the Course of Economic Development." *World Development,* vol. 1, no. 12 (December), pp. 29–36.

Hoffmann, P. G. 1960. *One Hundred Countries, One and One Quarter Billion People: How to Speed their Economic Growth and Ours in the 1960s.* Washington, D.C.: Committee for International Economic Growth.

Hoover, Calvin. 1946. "The Future of the German Economy." *American Economic Review,* vol. 36, no. 2 (May), pp. 642–49.

Horvat, Branko. 1974. "Welfare of the Common Man in Various Countries," *World Development,* vol. 2, no. 7 (July), pp. 29–39.

Hoselitz, Bert. 1956. "Non Economic Factors in Economic Development." *American Economic Review,* vol. 46, no. 2 (May), pp. 28–41.

Huang, Yukon. 1976. "Distribution of the Tax Burden in Tanzania." *Economic Journal,* vol. 86, no. 341 (March), pp. 73–86.

Hughes, Helen. 1976. "Industrialization and Development: A Stocktaking." Vienna: United Nations Industrial Development Organization.

Hulsman-Vejsová, Marie. 1975. "Misleading Official Exchange-Rate Conversions." *Economic Journal,* vol. 85, no. 337 (March), pp. 140–47.

International Food Policy Research Institute [IFPRI]. 1977. "Recent and Prospective Developments in Food Consumption: Some Policy Issues." New York: United Nations Protein-Calorie Advisory Group. Processed.

International Labour Office. 1961. *Employment Objectives in Economic Development.* Geneva.

————. 1970. *Towards Full Employment. A Programme For Colombia.* Geneva.

————. 1976. *Employment, Growth and Basic Needs.* Geneva.

————. 1976. *Tripartite World Conference on Employment, Income Distribution and Social Progress and the International Division of Labor: Background Papers.* Geneva.

————. 1977. *Meeting Basic Needs.* Geneva.

Johnson, D. Gale. 1976. "Increased Stability of Grain Supplies in Developing Countries: Optimal Carryovers and Insurance." *World Development,* vol. 4, no. 12 (December), pp. 977–88.

Johnson, Harry. 1965. "A Theoretical Model of Economic Nationalism in New and Developing States." *Political Science Quarterly,* vol. 80, no. 2 (June), pp. 169–85.

Jolly, Richard. 1976. "The World Employment Conference: The Enthronement of Basic Needs." *Overseas Development Institute* [ODI] *Review,* no. 2 (October), pp. 31–44.

Joshi, Heather, Harold Lubell, and Jean Mouly. 1976. *Abidjan: Urban Development and Employment in the Ivory Coast.* Geneva: International Labour Office.

Joy, Leonard. 1973. "Food and Nutrition Planning." *Journal of Agricultural Economics,* vol. 24, no. 1 (January), pp. 1–22.

Keesing, Donald. 1975. "Economic Lessons from China." *Journal of Development Economics,* vol. 2, no. 1 (June), pp. 1–32.

————. 1975a. "Mexican Education." Stanford, Calif.: Stanford University Economics Department. Processed.

————. 1977. "Employment and Lack of Employment in Mexico, 1900–70." In *Quantitative Latin American Studies, Statistical*

Abstract of Latin America, supplement 6. Edited by James Wilkie and Kenneth Ruddle. Los Angeles: U. C. L. A.

Khan, A. R. 1976. "Basic Needs: An Illustrative Exercise in Identification and Quantification with Respect to Bangladesh." Geneva: International Labour Office. Processed.

Kilby, Peter, ed. 1971. *Entrepreneurship and Economic Development.* New York: The Free Press.

Kleiman, Ephraim. 1976. "Trade and the Decline of Colonialism." *Economic Journal,* vol. 86, no. 343 (September), pp. 459–80.

Klein, Sidney. 1965. "Recent Economic Experience in India and Communist China: Another Interpretation." *American Economic Review,* vol. 55, no. 2 (May), pp. 31–39.

Klein, Thomas. 1972. "Economic Aid through Debt Relief." Washington, D.C.: World Bank. Processed.

Kravis, Irving B., Alan Heston, and Robert Summers. 1977. "Real GDP Per Capita for 116 Countries, 1970 and 1974." Department of Economics Discussion Paper no. 391. Philadelphia: University of Pennsylvania. Processed.

———. 1977a. "International Comparisons of Real Product and Purchasing Power." United Nations International Comparison Project, Phase II. Washington, D.C.: World Bank. Processed. Also forthcoming (1978) from The Johns Hopkins University Press.

Kravis, Irving B., and others. 1975. *A System of International Comparisons of Gross Product and Purchasing Power.* United Nations International Comparison Project, Phase I. Baltimore: Johns Hopkins University Press.

Kritz, Ernesto, and Joseph Ramos. 1976. "The Measurement of Urban Underemployment: A Report on Three Experimental Surveys." *International Labour Review,* vol. 113, no. 1 (January–February), pp. 115–27.

Krueger, Anne. 1978. *Foreign Trade Regimes and Economic Growth: Anatomy of Exchange Control.* New York: Ballinger, for the National Bureau of Economic Research.

Kumar, Dharma. 1974. "Changes in Income Distribution and Poverty in India: A Review of the Literature." *World Development,* vol. 2, no. 1 (January), pp. 31–41.

Kuznets, Simon. 1955. "Economic Growth and Income Inequality." *American Economic Review,* vol. 45, no. 1 (March), pp. 1–28.

———. 1963. "Quantitative Aspects of the Economic Growth of

Nations: VIII. Distribution of Income by Size." *Economic Development and Cultural Change,* vol. 11, no. 2, part II (January), pp. 1–37.

————. 1965. *Economic Growth and Structure.* New York: W. W. Norton.

————. 1967. *Modern Economic Growth.* New Haven: Yale University Press.

————. 1971. *Economic Growth of Nations.* Cambridge, Mass.: Harvard University Press.

————. 1972. "The Gap: Concept, Measurement, Trends." In *The Gap Between Rich and Poor Nations.* By Gustav Ranis. London: Macmillan.

————. 1972a. "Problems in Comparing Recent Growth Rates for Developed and Less Developed Countries." *Economic Development and Cultural Change,* vol. 20, no. 2 (January), pp. 185–209.

Lal, Deepak. 1976. "Distribution and Development: A Review Article." *World Development,* vol. 4, no. 9 (September), pp. 725–38.

Langoni, Carlos. 1973. *Distribuição de Rendas e Desenvolvimento Econômico do Brasil.* Rio de Janeiro: Editora Expressao e Cultura.

Lappé, Frances Moore and Joseph Collins. 1976. *Food First: Beyond the Myth of Scarcity.* New York: Houghton Mifflin.

Lehmann, David. 1977. "The Death of Land Reform." Paper read at the World Bank Workshop on Analysis of Distributional Issues in Development Planning, April 22–27 at Bellagio, Italy. Processed.

Leibenstein, Harvey. 1957. *Economic Backwardness and Economic Growth.* New York: John Wiley.

Lewis, W. Arthur. 1954. "Economic Development with Unlimited Supplies of Labor." *Manchester School,* vol. 22, no. 2 (May), pp. 139–91.

————. 1955. *The Theory of Economic Growth.* Homewood, Ill.: Richard D. Irwin.

————. 1965. "A Review of Economic Development," vol. 55, no. 2 (May), pp. 1–16.

————. 1972. "Objectives and Prognostications." In *The Gap Between Rich and Poor Nations.* By Gustav Ranis. London: Macmillan.

Lipton, Michael. 1972. "Aid Allocation When Aid Is Inadequate:

Problems of Non-Implementation of the Pearson Report." In *Foreign Resources and Economic Development: A Symposium on the Report of the Pearson Commission.* Edited by T. J. Byers. London: Frank Cass.

————. 1977. *Why Poor People Stay Poor: A Study of Urban Bias in World Development.* London: Temple Smith.

Little, I. M. D. 1976. "Book Review" (of Adelman and Morris, 1973, and Chenery and others, 1974). *Journal of Development Economics,* vol. 3, no. 1 (June), pp. 99–116.

————, Tibor Scitovsky, and Maurice Scott. 1970. *Industry and Trade in Some Developing Countries: A Comparative Study.* London: Oxford University Press.

Lydall, Harold. 1977. "Income Distribution During the Process of Development." ILO World Employment Program, Income Distribution and Employment Program Working Paper, no. 52. Geneva: International Labour Office.

————. 1977a. "Unemployment in Developing Countries." Income Distribution and Employment Program Working Paper, no. 50. Geneva: ILO World Employment Program.

Lysy, Frank, and Lance Taylor. 1977. "A Computable General Equilibrium Model for the Functional Income Distribution: Experiments for Brazil, 1959–71." Washington, D.C.: World Bank. Processed.

Maddison, Angus. 1970. *Economic Progress and Policy in Developing Countries.* New York: W. W. Norton.

Malenbaum, Wilfred. 1959. "India and China: Contrasts in Development." *American Economic Review,* vol. 49, no. 3 (June), pp. 284–309.

Maliyamkono, T. L. 1976. "Educational Reform for Development: A Review of the Tanzanian Approach." Washington, D.C.: World Bank. Processed.

Mandelbaum, K. 1945. *The Industrialization of Backward Areas.* Oxford: Basil Blackwell.

Mansour, Fawzy. 1977. "Third World Revolt and Self-Reliant Auto-Centered Strategy of Development." Paper read to the Working Group for the Third Colloquium, Rothko Chapel. Houston. Processed.

Mazumdar, Dipak. 1975. "The Urban Informal Sector." World Bank Staff Working Paper, no. 211. Washington, D.C.: World Bank.

McClelland, David. 1961. *The Achieving Society.* New York: Van Nostrand.

McGranahan, Donald. 1972. "Development Indicators and Development Models." *Journal of Development Studies,* vol. 8, no. 3 (April), pp. 91–102.

Meerman, Jacob. 1972. "Fiscal Incidence in Empirical Studies of Income Distribution in Poor Countries." Washington, D.C.: U.S. Agency for International Development, Discussion Paper no. 25. Processed.

Meier, Gerald. 1976. *Leading Issues in Economic Development,* 3rd ed. New York: Oxford University Press.

Mikesell, Raymond. 1954. "Economic Doctrines Reflected in UN Reports." *American Economic Review,* vol. 44, no. 2 (May), pp. 570–82.

Minhas, B. S. 1977. "Self-reliance and India's Planning Strategy." Paper read to the Working Group for the Third Colloquium, Rothko Chapel. Houston. Processed.

Morawetz, David. 1974. "Employment Implications of Industrialization: A Survey." *Economic Journal,* vol. 84, no. 335 (September), pp. 491–542.

————. 1974a. *The Andean Group: A Case Study in Economic Integration Among Developing Countries.* Cambridge, Mass.: M.I.T. Press.

————. 1978. "Castro Market: Slices of Economic Life in a Poor Chilean Fishing Town." *World Development* 6 (forthcoming).

————, and others. 1977. "The Income Distribution and Self-rated Happiness: Some Empirical Evidence." *Economic Journal,* vol. 87, no. 347 (September), pp. 511–22.

Musgrove, Philip. 1976. "Distribution, Development, and Integration in Latin America: Five Propositions." Washington, D.C.: Brookings Institution. Processed.

Myint, Hla. 1964. *The Economics of the Developing Countries.* London: Hutchinson.

Myrdal, Gunnar. 1957. *Economic Theory and Underdeveloped Regions.* London: Gerald Duckworth.

Nafziger, E. W. 1975. "Class Caste and Community of South Indian Industrialists: An Examination of the Horatio Alger Model." *Journal of Development Studies,* vol. 11, no. 2 (January), pp. 131–48.

————. 1977. "Entrepreneurship, Social Mobility, and Income Redistribution in South India." *American Economic Review,* vol. 67, no. 1 (February), pp. 76–80.

Naseem, S. M. 1977. "Rural Poverty and Landlessness in Pakistan:

Dimensions and Trends." World Employment Program, paper, no. 10–6/WP–14. Geneva: International Labour Office.

Norbye, Ole. 1976. "Planning to Meet 'Basic Needs': Some Methodological Problems and Research Opportunities." Department of Economic Research and Problems, no. 76. Bergen, Norway: The Chr. Michelsen Institute.

Oftedal, Olav, and F. James Levinson. 1974. "Health, Nutrition and Income Distribution." International Nutrition Planning Program. Cambridge, Mass.: M.I.T. Processed.

Pant, Pitambar. 1962. "Perspective of Development: 1961–1976, Implications of Planning for a Minimum Level of Living." In *Poverty and Income Distribution in India*. Edited by T. Srinivasan and P. K. Bardhan. Calcutta: Statistical Publishing Society.

Papanek, Gustav. 1962. "The Development of Entrepreneurship." *American Economic Review,* vol. 52, no. 2 (May), pp. 46–58.

———. 1975. "Growth, Income Distribution, and Politics in Less Developed Countries." In *Economic Growth in Developing Countries*. Edited by Yohanan Ramati. New York: Praeger.

Paukert, Felix. 1973. "Income Distribution at Different Levels of Development: A Survey of Evidence." *International Labour Review,* vol. 108, no. 2 (August), pp. 97–125.

Pearson, Lester, and others. 1969. *Partners in Development: Report of the Commission on International Development*. New York: Praeger.

Penny, David, and Terry McGee. 1975. "Some Comments on H. W. Arndt's 'Development and Equality: The Indonesian Case'." Canberra: Australian National University, School of Pacific Studies. Processed.

Pigou, A. C. 1912. *Wealth and Welfare*. London: Macmillan.

———. 1920. *The Economics of Welfare*. London: Macmillan.

Pugwash Symposium. 1977. "The Role of Self-Reliance in Alternative Strategies for Development." *World Development,* vol. 5, no. 3 (March), pp. 257–65.

Pyatt, Graham. 1977. "On International Comparisons of Income Inequality." *American Economic Review,* vol. 67, no. 1 (February), pp. 71–75.

Ramati, Yohanan, ed. 1975. *Economic Growth in Developing Countries*. New York: Praeger.

Ramos, Joseph. 1974. "An Heterodoxical Interpretation of the Employment Problem in Latin America." *World Development,* vol. 2, no. 7 (July), pp. 47–58.

Ranis, Gustav. 1962. "International Aid for Underdeveloped Countries: A Comment." *Review of Economics and Statistics,* vol. 44, no. 4 (November), pp. 484–86.

————. 1972. *The Gap Between Rich and Poor Nations.* London: Macmillan.

————. 1975. "LDC Employment and Growth: A Synthesis of Economic Growth Center Research." Yale University Economic Growth Center Discussion Paper, no. 231. New Haven.

————. 1976. "Development Theory at Three Quarters Century." Yale University Economic Growth Center Discussion Paper, no. 242. New Haven.

————. 1977. "Equity with Growth in Taiwan: How 'Special' is the 'Special Case'?" New Haven: Yale University Economic Growth Center. Processed.

Rao, D. C. 1978. "Economic Growth and Equity in The Republic of Korea." *World Development,* vol. 6, no. 3, pp. 383–96.

Renaud, Bertrand. 1976. "Economic Growth and Income Inequality in Korea." World Bank Staff Working Paper, no. 240. Washington, D.C.: World Bank.

Reutlinger, Shlomo, and Marcelo Selowsky. 1976. *Malnutrition and Poverty: Magnitude and Policy Options.* Baltimore: Johns Hopkins University Press.

Richards, Peter. 1977. "Underemployment and Basic Needs Satisfaction." ILO World Employment Program Working Paper, no. 48. Geneva: International Labour Office.

Robbins, Lionel. 1968. *The Theory of Economic Development in the History of Economic Thought.* London: Macmillan.

Roemer, Michael. 1977. "Resource-Based Industrialization in the Developing Countries, A Survey of the Literature." Harvard Institute for International Development Discussion Paper, no. 21. Cambridge, Mass.

Rosenstein-Rodan, Paul. 1943. "Problems of Industrialization of Eastern and South-Eastern Europe." *Economic Journal,* no. 53 (June–September), pp. 202–11.

————. 1961. "International Aid for Underdeveloped Countries." *Review of Economics and Statistics,* vol. 43, no. 2 (May), pp. 107–38.

Rothstein, Robert. 1976. "The Political Economy of Redistribution and Self-Reliance." *World Development,* vol. 4, no. 7 (July), pp. 593–611.

Ruderman, A. P. 1977. "What Does the PQLI Really Measure?" *International Development Review,* vol. 19, no. 1, p. 38.

Sarris, Alexander, and Lance Taylor. 1976. "Cereal Stocks, Food Aid, and Food Security for the Poor." *World Development,* vol. 4, no. 12 (December), pp. 967–76.

Saunders, Robert, and Jeremy Warford. 1976. *Village Water Supply: Economics and Policy in the Developing World.* Baltimore: Johns Hopkins University Press.

Schumpeter, Joseph. 1936. *The Theory of Economic Development.* Cambridge, Mass.: Harvard University Press.

Seers, Dudley. 1972. "What Are We Trying to Measure?" *Journal of Development Studies,* vol. 8, no. 3 (April), pp. 21–36.

Selowsky, Marcelo, and Lance Taylor. 1973. "The Economics of Malnourished Children: An Example of Disinvestment in Human Capital." *Economic Development and Cultural Change,* vol. 22, no. 1 (October), pp. 17–30.

Sen, Amartya. 1973. *On Economic Inequality.* Oxford: Clarendon Press.

————. 1976. "Economic Development: Objectives and Obstacles." Paper presented at the SSRC–ACLS Conference on the Lessons of China's Development Experience for the Developing Countries, San Juan, Puerto Rico.

Sewell, John, and the Overseas Development Council. 1977. *The United States and World Development: Agenda 77.* New York: Praeger.

Sharpston, Michael. 1972. "Uneven Geographical Distribution of Medical Care: a Ghanaian Case Study." *Journal of Development Studies,* vol. 8, no. 2 (January), pp. 205–22.

————. c. 1975. "Health: Searching for a Viable Policy." Washington, D.C.: World Bank. Processed.

————. n.d. "Factors Determining the Health Situation in Developing Countries." Washington, D.C.: World Bank. Processed.

Shell, Karl, ed. 1967. *Essays on the Theory of Optimal Economic Growth.* Cambridge, Mass.: M.I.T. Press.

Simmons, John, and others. Forthcoming. *The Education Dilemma: Policy Issues for Developing Countries.* Oxford: Pergammon.

Sinha, Radha. 1976. *Food and Poverty*. London: Croom Helm.

Srinivasan, T. N. 1977. "Development Policies and Levels of Living of the Poor: Some Issues." Report of the World Bank Workshop on Analysis of Distributional Issues in Development Planning, April 22–27 at Bellagio, Italy. Processed.

————, and P. K. Bardhan, eds. 1974. *Poverty and Income Distribution in India*. Calcutta: Statistical Publishing Society.

Staley, Eugene. 1954. *The Future of Underdeveloped Countries*. New York: Harper Brothers.

Stewart, Frances. 1977. "Inequality, Technology, and Payments Systems." Paper presented at the World Bank Workshop on Analysis of Distributional Issues in Development Planning, April 22–27 at Bellagio, Italy. Processed.

————, and Paul Streeten. 1976. "New Strategies for Development: Poverty, Income Distribution, and Growth." *Quarterly Journal of Economics,* vol. 28, no. 3 (November), pp. 381–405.

Streeten, Paul. 1972. "Technology Gaps Between Rich and Poor Countries." In *The Frontiers of Development Studies*. New York: John Wiley.

————. 1972a. *The Frontiers of Development Studies*. New York: John Wiley.

————. 1977. "Basic Needs." Washington, D.C.: World Bank. Processed.

————. 1977a. "A Survey of Some Ideas about Development." Paper presented to the Working Group for the Third Colloquium, Rothko Chapel. Houston. Processed.

————. 1977b. "The Distinctive Features of a Basic Needs Approach to Development." Washington, D.C.: World Bank. Processed.

Strout, Alan. 1977. "The Future of Nuclear Power in Developing Countries." M.I.T. Energy Laboratory Working Paper, no. 77–006. Cambridge, Mass.: M.I.T.

Sunkel, Osvaldo. 1969. "National Development Policy and External Dependence in Latin America." *Journal of Development Studies,* vol. 6, no. 1 (October), pp. 23–48.

Tannebaum, Gerald, and John Simmons. 1977. "Educational Reform in China." Washington, D.C.: World Bank. Processed.

Taylor, Lance. 1975. "The Misconstrued Crisis: Lester Brown and World Food." *World Development,* vol. 3, no. 11 (November), pp. 827–37.

Taylor, Lance, and Frank Lysy. 1977. "Vanishing Short-run Income Redistributions: Keynesian Clues About Model Surprises." Paper read at the World Bank Workshop on Analysis of Distributional Issues in Development Planning, April 22–27 at Bellagio, Italy. Processed.

Thorbecke, Erik. 1973. "The Employment Problem: A Critical Evaluation of Four ILO Comprehensive Country Reports." *International Labour Review,* vol. 107, no. 5 (May), pp. 393–424.

Thorp, Willard. 1951. "Some Basic Policy Issues in Economic Development." *American Economic Review,* vol. 41, no. 2 (May), pp. 407–17.

Timmer, C. Peter. 1976. "Food Policy in China." *Food Research Institute Studies,* vol. 15, no. 1, pp. 53–69.

Tinbergen, Jan. 1975. *Income Distribution: Analysis and Policies.* Amsterdam: North-Holland.

———, and others. 1976. *Rio: Reshaping the International Order.* New York: E. P. Dutton.

Tobin, James, and William Nordhaus. 1972. *Economic Growth.* General Series no. 96, vol. 5. New York: Columbia University Press and the National Bureau of Economic Research.

Turnham, David. 1971. *The Employment Problem in Less Developed Countries.* Paris: Organization for Economic Cooperation and Development.

Tyler, William. 1976. "Brazilian Industrialization and Industrial Policies: A Survey." *World Development,* vol. 4, no. 10 (October), pp. 863–82.

United Nations. 1974. *Assessment of the World Food Situation: Present and Future.* Rome: United Nations World Food Conference, E/Conf.65/3.

———. 1975. *Poverty, Unemployment and Development Policy: A Case Study of Selected Issues with Reference to Kerala.* New York: United Nations Department of Economic and Social Affairs, ST/ESA/29.

———. 1975a. "Selected Demographic Indicators by Countries 1950–2000." New York: United Nations Department for Economic and Social Affairs, ESA/P/WP.55. Processed.

———. 1975b. "Developing Countries and Levels of Development." New York: United Nations, E/AC.54/L.81.

———. 1976. "The Future of the World Economy." New York: United Nations Department of Economic and Social Affairs. Processed.

United Nations Research Institute for Social Development. 1966. *The Level of Living Index.* Geneva.

―――. 1970. *Contents and Measurement of Socio-Economic Development: An Empirical Enquiry.* Geneva.

Uphoff, N. E., and W. F. Ilchman. 1972. *The Political Economy of Development.* Berkeley: University of California Press.

Usher, Dan. 1968. *The Price Mechanism and the Meaning of National Income Statistics.* Oxford: Clarendon Press.

Viner, Jacob. 1952. *International Trade and Economic Development.* Glencoe, Ill.: The Free Press.

Warren, Bill. 1977. "The Postwar Economic Experience of the Third World." Paper read to the Working Group of the Third Colloquium, Rothko Chapel. Houston. Processed.

Watanabe, Susumu. 1970. "Entrepreneurship in Small Enterprises in Japanese Manufacturing." *International Labour Review,* vol. 102, no. 6 (December), pp. 531–76.

Webb, Richard. 1977. *Government Policy and the Distribution of Income in Peru, 1963–73.* Cambridge, Mass.: Harvard University Press.

Weisskoff, Richard, and Adolfo Figueroa. 1976. "Traversing the Social Pyramid: A Comparative Review of Income Distribution in Latin America." *Latin American Research Review,* vol. 11, no. 2, pp. 71–112.

Weisskopf, Thomas. 1972. "Capitalism, Underdevelopment, and the Future of the Poor Countries." *Review of Radical Political Economics,* vol. 4, no. 1 (Spring), pp. 1–35.

―――. 1975. "China and India: Contrasting Experiences in Economic Development." *American Economic Review,* vol. 65, no. 2 (May), pp. 356–64.

Westphal, Larry. 1977. "Korea's Experience with Export-Led Industrial Development." World Bank Staff Working Paper, no. 249. Washington, D.C.: World Bank. Processed.

Wilber, C. K., ed. 1973. *The Political Economy of Development and Underdevelopment.* New York: Random.

Wilkie, James, and Kenneth Ruddle, eds. 1977. *Quantitative Latin American Studies, Statistical Abstract of Latin America,* supplement 6, Los Angeles: U.C.L.A.

World Bank. 1950. *The Basis of a Development Program for Colombia.* Washington, D.C.

―――. 1973. "Nutrition and Health of Indonesian Construction

Workers: Endurance and Anaemia." World Bank Staff Working Paper, no. 152. Washington, D.C.

————. 1974. *Population Policies and Economic Development.* Washington, D.C.

————. 1974a. *Education: Sector Working Paper.* Washington, D.C.

————. 1975. *Health: Sector Policy Paper.* Washington, D.C.

————. 1975a. *Housing: Sector Policy Paper.* Washington, D.C.

————. 1976. "Urban Poverty and Employment." Draft Issues Paper. Washington, D.C. Processed.

————. 1976a. *World Tables 1976.* Baltimore: Johns Hopkins University Press.

————. 1977. "Basic Needs: An Issues Paper." Washington, D.C. Processed.

————. 1977a. "The External Debt of Developing Countries." Washington, D.C. Processed.

Wortman, Sterling, and others. 1976. "Food and Agriculture." *Scientific American,* vol. 235, no. 3 (September), pp. 30–205.

Yotopoulos, Pan, and Jeffrey Nugent. 1976. *Economics and Development: Empirical Investigations.* New York: Harper and Row.